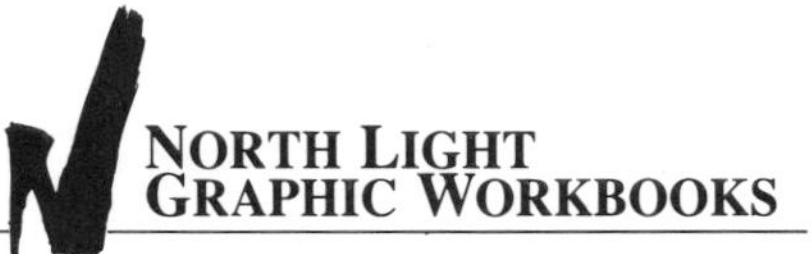

Marker Techniques

ILLUSTRATION WORKBOOK 4

Lee Woolery

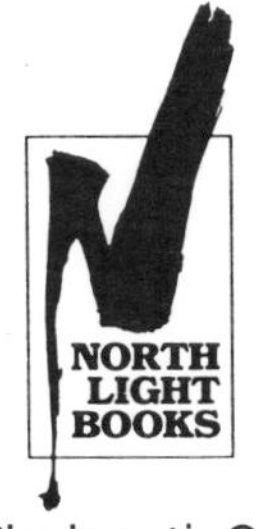

Cincinnati, Ohio

 Published by North Light Books, an imprint of F&W Publications, Inc., 1507 Dana Avenue, Cincinnati, Ohio 45207. First edition.

ISBN 0-89134-237-0

Concept and editorial development by Diana Martin
Interior design by Carol Buchanan

INTRODUCTION

Illustration is the ultimate means of expression for many graphic artists. If it's the kind of artistic challenge you're aching to take on, here's your chance. Armed with a variety of marker skills, you're now ready to tackle full-blown, complex renderings similar to those that professional illustrators handle every day.

Don't be intimidated by the complexity of these subjects. They may look hard, but they're rendered using techniques you already know. Each will help you explore further uses for art markers. Each will demand acute observational skills, but then you've learned the importance of studying every form you render. Each will remind you that successful marker rendering doesn't just happen—it requires thought, practiced skills, and, of course, talent.

Having completed Workbooks 1, 2, and 3, you are now ready to bring all of these elements together in exciting marker illustrations.

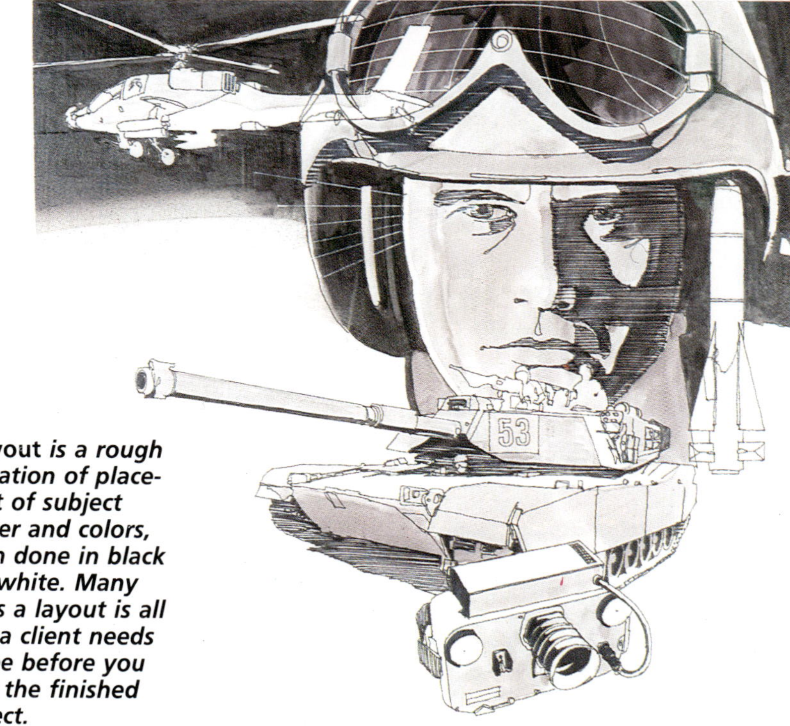

A layout is a rough indication of placement of subject matter and colors, often done in black and white. Many times a layout is all that a client needs to see before you start the finished project.

The Series

To complete this workbook, the fourth in the *Marker Techniques* series, it's absolutely necessary that you know the principles and skills taught in the first three workbooks. If you feel at all unsure about any marker rendering technique, go back to the appropriate workbook and refresh your memory. If you haven't completed an earlier workbook, do so before proceeding any further with this book.

As in the previous workbooks, in this one you'll continue to *participate*. Projects will feature step-by-step demonstrations and instructional captions that show you the mechanics of each technique, as well as the way different rendering methods can be combined. After you've studied the how-to's of each project, turn to the practice pages following the last demonstration and begin!

You'll find multiple practice pages for each project; the drawings' outlines are preprinted, which frees you to concentrate solely on rendering. Some have guidelines for you to follow that indicate contour areas, highlights, shadows, and/or details. These should help you capture a subject's unique look.

Illustrating with Markers

Markers can be used to render any subject from wildlife to high-tech machinery. As a professional illustrator, you'll find markers are without equal when it comes to speed, range of color, and ease of application. Yet their commercial use is limited. As a general rule, most clients want a final illustration to be painted, not rendered in marker. So no matter how proficient you become, marker rendering will always be a secondary skill.

With this in mind, I would hasten to add that this secondary skill is nonetheless very valuable. Virtually every art studio and ad agency needs quick layouts and comps, the bulk of which are done in marker. As you learned in Workbooks 1 and 3, a *layout* is a rendering that shows a client basically what will appear in a final illustration. It shows faces, details, and other refinements. A *comp* (comprehen-

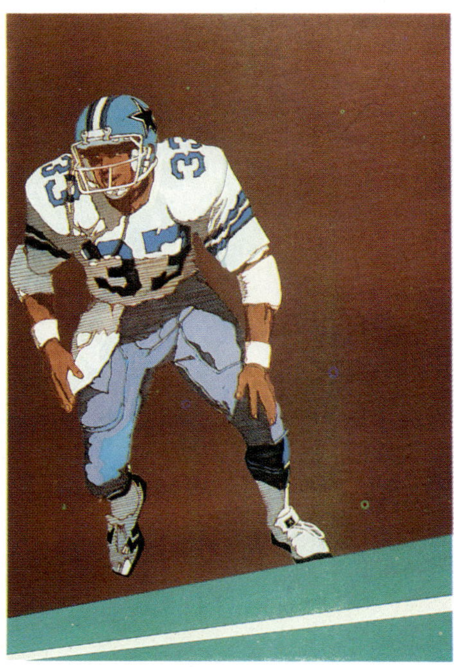

In contrast a comp is a marker rendering that shows very much what the final image will look like. The comp is especially needed on large-budget jobs where the client wants a close indication of how the final will look before it is begun.

In this reference photo and its final rendering, you can see how the basic light and dark structures are the same. Notice how the illustration captures the feeling of movement. You don't want to copy exactly what you see in a photograph—add your own artistic interpretation!

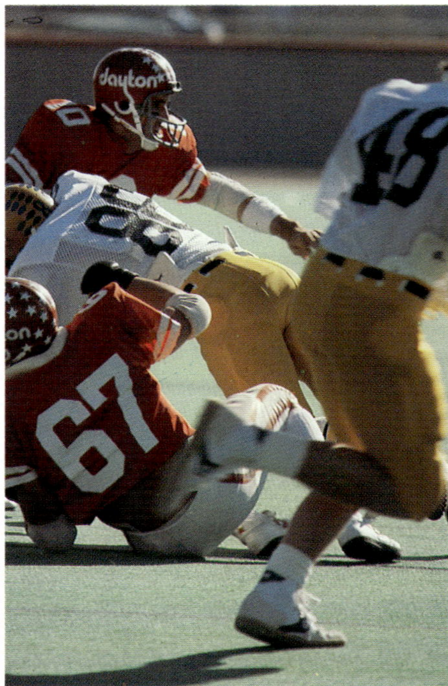

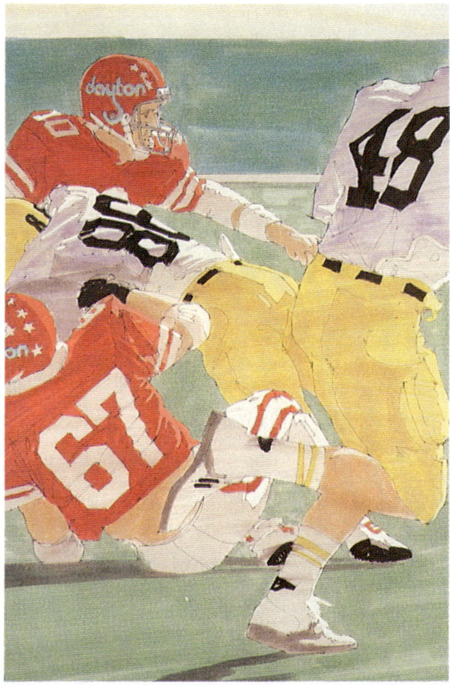

sive) is a rendering that shows artwork almost as it would appear in final form, without investing the time or expense in actually doing a final. Comps are used when a client wishes to see how a finished illustration will look before spending money on printing or color separations. They also give an art director the opportunity to make changes before the final. Since it's always easier to make changes in the earlier stages of a project, you can see how marker renderings are a valuable component in the total creative process.

The projects featured in this workbook could be used as layouts or even comps, because of their degree of finish. If you were to do a marker rendering of this complexity before a final, it would make illustrating the final in other mediums much simpler. And if you were to present a client with a layout or comp to this degree of finish, it would give the client much more confidence in your ability to do an outstanding final illustration.

Working from References

The projects in this workbook were drawn from either reference photos or slides. Because marker rendering is so precise, you usually need visual references to get the proper look, the proper feeling. I took the pictures of these subjects myself in order to get just the right lighting and perspective.

My reference shots are usually taken with a Polaroid camera so I can quickly see how the lighting and positioning look. With a Polaroid, you can check these things within 60 seconds and make your adjustments on the spot. You can certainly use a 35mm camera for this purpose, but you won't know how your shots turn out until they're back from the lab a day or two later. If they're not what you want, you have to reshoot the scene, which will cost you both time and money.

The most popular means of gathering references is to clip photos from magazines. You place them in folders and file them according to category. Then when you need a shot from a specific category, you have it at your fingertips. Be sure to use other artists' works *only* as general references; if you copy an image you may find yourself facing a lawsuit and charges of copyright infringement.

Preparing Your Drawings

Once you complete this workbook, you should begin generating drawings from reference material that can be used as the basis for marker renderings.

Waterproof fine-line markers work the best for marker drawings. Unlike pencil, charcoal, or pastels, the ink will not smear when marker is applied. Also, the lines are very fine and will be concealed as more color is applied. My personal favorites are the Razor Point series by Pilot and the Niji Stylist pens. Both offer very fine lines and are great to draw with. The black Pilot Razor Point is best for dark-toned objects or portions of an illustration that will be later outlined. The gray Niji Stylist is good for paler areas, those that will be rendered in medium-to-light values. Two or three layers of pigment can completely conceal a fine Niji line.

You must simplify the drawings by eliminating all unnecessary features. Some linework can be used as a guide for highlights and shadows, but when you first begin doing your own drawings, keep them as simple as possible and concentrate on the most important parts. When you're drawing anything artifical, like a building or a car, be sure to use a straightedge, French curves, and ellipse guides to ensure accuracy.

A professional illustrator may use a projector or a camera lucida to speed up the drawing process. The image is blown up on a wall or down on a drawing board, then you draw the areas that you think are necessary. You, as the graphic artist, decide which lines will stay and which will go. When you do this, be careful not to fall into the category of a tracer. You must be able to draw before using *any* kind of projector. Remember, these are simply devices to speed up the process; they should not be used as a substitute for drawing ability.

Selecting Paper

Obviously your drawing will be done on paper, but what kind? The paper you choose is as important as your choice of marker. There are some twenty different brands of paper specially made for marker use. My choice is the Aquabee Series 633 marker paper because it retains the color's accuracy and keeps bleed to a minimum. Some papers will bleed a great deal but give you very accurate color. Others will bleed very little, but color is muted and almost pastel in intensity.

In my opinion, it's better to use a paper that bleeds but retains color intensity. You'll learn to control bleed much quicker with this paper. A paper that bleeds a great deal allows you more time to blend and glaze colors because it takes longer for the pigment to dry. The other type of paper will absorb the pigment too quickly, leaving hardly any time for blending. As you can see, the paper is an integral part of marker rendering. I would suggest choosing a paper the same way you would a marker: try a few samples at an art supply store to find the one that best suits your needs.

The practice paper provided in this workbook does allow some color to bleed through. You should place a piece of typing paper beneath each practice page. Also be aware that the Berol broad nib marker bleeds slightly more than the fine. It's best to keep the broad nib 1/16 inch away from the drawn lines and the fine nib 1/32 inch. A marker's age, color, and nib pressure can affect this measurement.

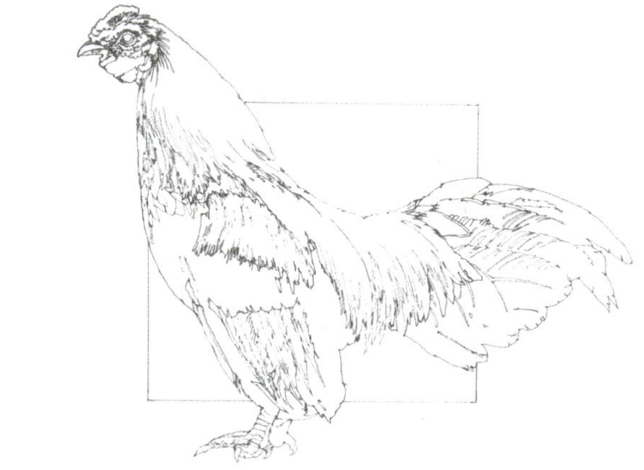

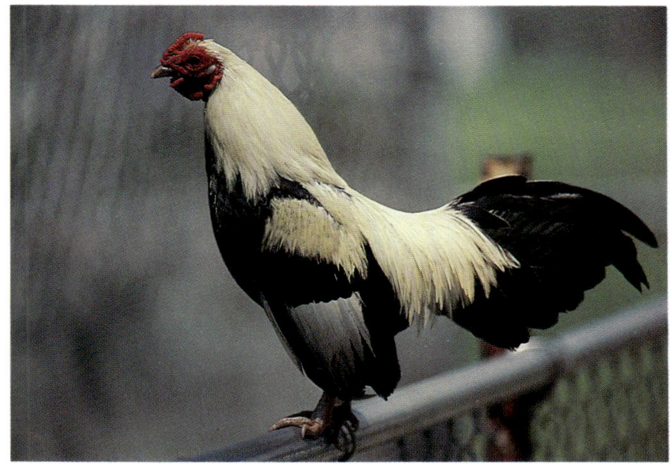

Study this drawing of the rooster to see how the form in the reference photo has been simplified for marker rendering. When you compare it to the photograph, you can see how many areas of the entire image were either left out or translated into simple line work. With complicated subjects like this, you must choose to leave in only those lines that are vital to the finished look.

The Projects

With this workbook you'll do marker illustrations of three distinctly different forms: a rooster, a football action scene, and a sports car. Each of these projects allows you to explore the different uses for art markers. Each is a bit more complicated, colorful, and detailed than the projects in earlier workbooks. And each demands you use every skill and bit of information acquired throughout this series.

The rooster, your first project, could be a cover comp for a brochure selling farm animal feed, or perhaps a poster for a morning television show. Since he's covered with feathers, you'll use the texture rendering techniques taught in Workbook 3. To capture the brilliant red of his wattle, you'll need to glaze on color, something you learned in Workbook 1. You'll use another technique taught in the first book, laying in flat color, for the smooth blue background.

Imagine doing a poster layout for your favorite professional football team or illustrating the cover for their weekly program. You'll get a feel for that type of work with the second project, a football action scene. Here you'll evoke the excitement of a game through bright colors and the interplay of lights and darks. Both elements add mood and drama to your illustration. In addition to the rendering methods you've already learned, this project introduces two new techniques: rendering over a medium-tone background and the use of paints other than white for highlights.

A shiny red sports car is the final project. This illustration could be a comp for a photo shoot or a project prototype rendering for an automobile manufacturer. With its bright, highly polished appearance, the car looks like it was just driven off the showroom floor. This illustration will tap all of the skills

Supplies You'll Need

Markers: For this workbook you'll need five Berol Prismacolor double-nibbed warm grays (10%, 20%, 40%, 50%, and 60%) and four cool grays (10%, 30%, 50%, and 70%), plus the following colors: cream, beige, brick white, light flesh, apple blossom, scarlet lake, cranberry, grape, nonphoto blue, light violet, lime green, canary yellow, orange, and black. A Berol marker, with a nib on each end (one broad and the other fine) lets you render large areas and small without changing markers.

Other Materials: To complete these three projects you'll need a white Prismacolor pencil, a straightedge, a French curve, a no. 0 sable brush, Dr. Martin's Bleed Proof White, plus Winsor & Newton designer's gouache in brilliant yellow and grenadine.

PROJECT 1

RENDERING NATURE'S COLOR AND DETAIL

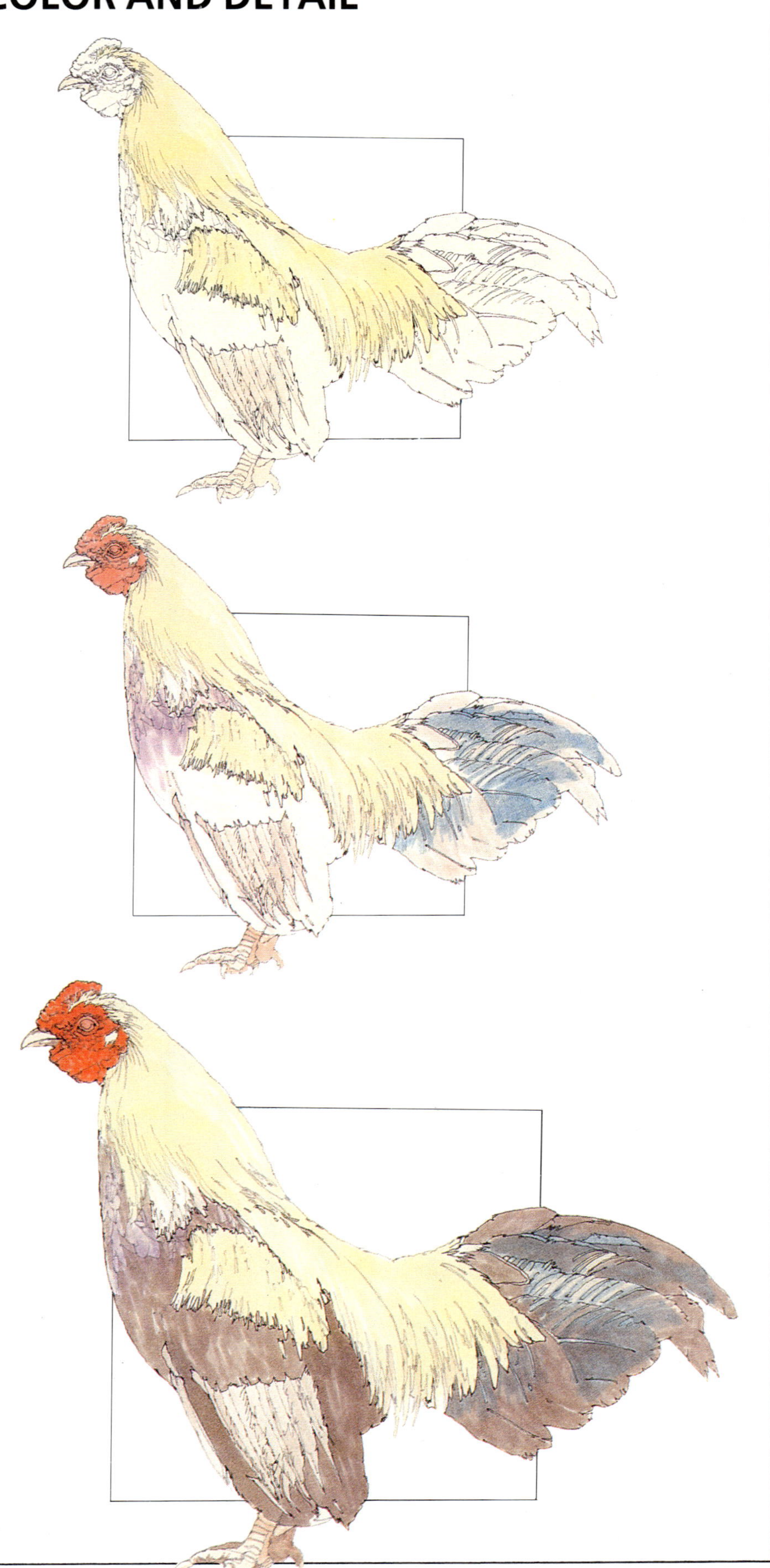

Step 1: To capture this rooster's brilliance and texture, you must apply pigment in layers, gradually building up the color and details. You'll be rendering lots of small areas, so use only fine-point markers. 1) First pull out the full-page reproduction of this image that follows Project 3. Begin by applying light flesh to the beak and feet.
2) Stroke cream over his neck, back, upper wing, and tail feathers.
3) Watching the bleed, cover the wing feathers with a layer of warm 10% gray.

Step 2: 1) Fill in the wattle with apple blossom, keeping color away from the beak and feathers around the head.
2) To indicate the tail feathers in shadow, apply warm 20% gray with a light stroke. 3) Some of the feathers have an iridescent quality; you'll indicate this with nonphoto blue on the tail. Apply the blue with short, choppy strokes that look like feathers and that follow the tail's direction. 4) Apply light violet to the breast feathers.
5) Stroke in beige under the beak and lightly on the legs to indicate shadows.

Step 3: 1) Continue building up color intensity on the wattle by dotting in two layers of scarlet lake. Dot the color on in a way that shows skin texture, letting some of the apple blossom base show through. Place your dots closer together in the shadows. 2) Darken the shadows under the beak and on the back side of the legs with warm 50% gray. Lay in a warm 50% gray undercoat along the breast, wing, and tail feathers. Use your line drawing as a guide for filling in around the violet feathers. Again, put the color on with strokes that look, and flow, like real feathers.

PROJECT 1: CONTINUED

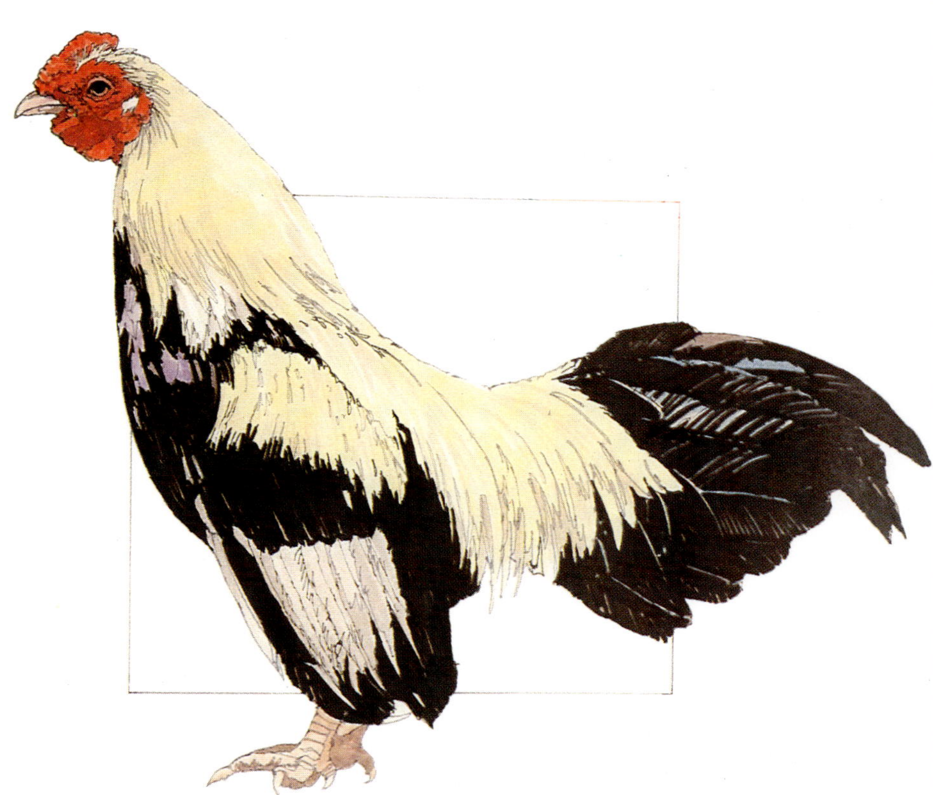

Step 4: 1) Carefully dot in shadows on the wattle with cranberry. 2) Fill in the pupil and around the top of the eyelid with black. Then apply black to the tail, wing, and breast with strokes that follow the direction of the feathers. Be sure to allow some of the warm 50% gray to show through, especially in highlighted areas. 3) Lay warm 20% gray on the lower wing feathers.
4) Apply another layer of light flesh to the beak and feet.

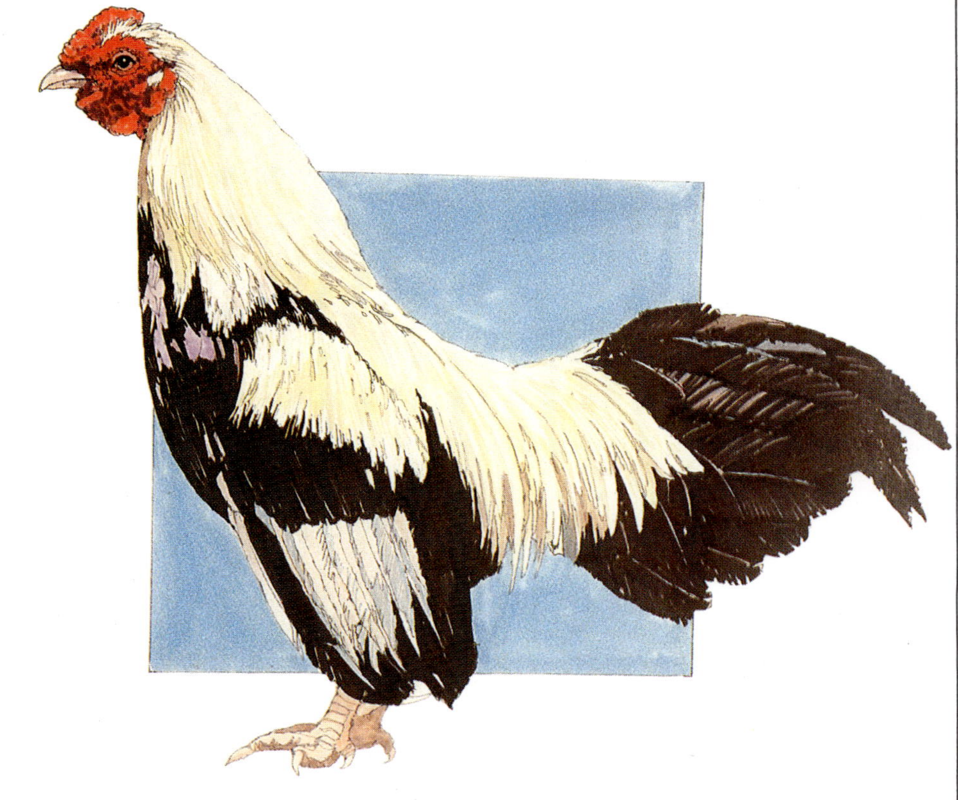

Step 5: 1) Apply a shadow of nonphoto blue to wing feathers. Next, with the same marker, fill the background square with flat blue; use a fine point to strike your boundary lines, then fill in with a broad nib. The square must be filled with a smooth layer of color so as not to detract from the subject.
2) To deepen shadows on the white tail feathers, stroke on warm 40% gray. Indicate shadow on the front of the breast with this same color.
3) Carefully dot on the wattle's deepest shadows in grape. These dots go over your earlier layers of cranberry.
4) To knock back the intensity of blue on the tail feathers, run one layer of warm 40% gray over this area.
5) Finish by painting in the white feathers with Dr. Martin's Bleed Proof White and a no. 0 sable brush. The brushstrokes should follow the direction of the feathers. Finally, dot in the eye highlight.

PROJECT 2

CAPTURING SPORTS IN ACTION

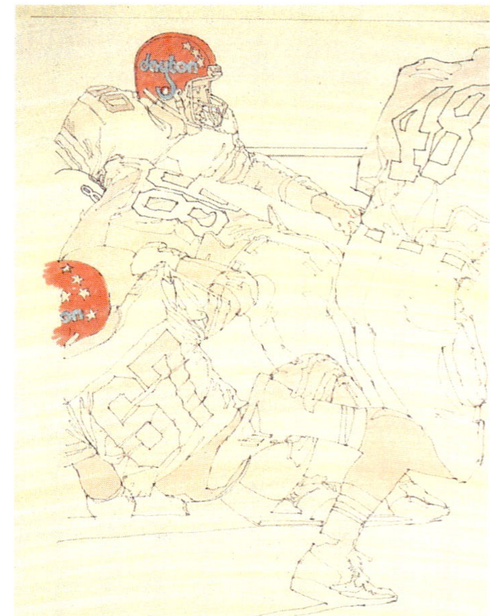

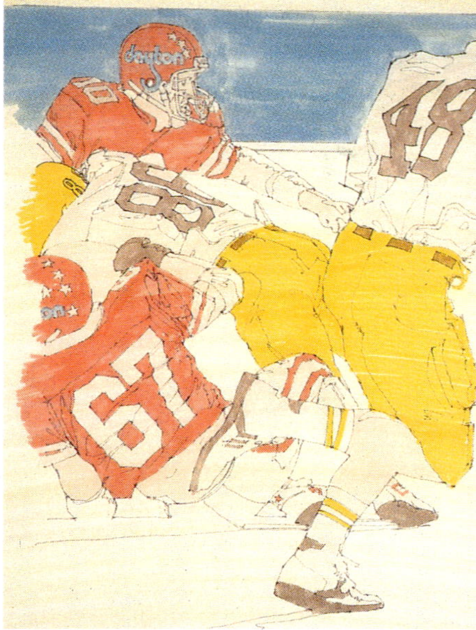

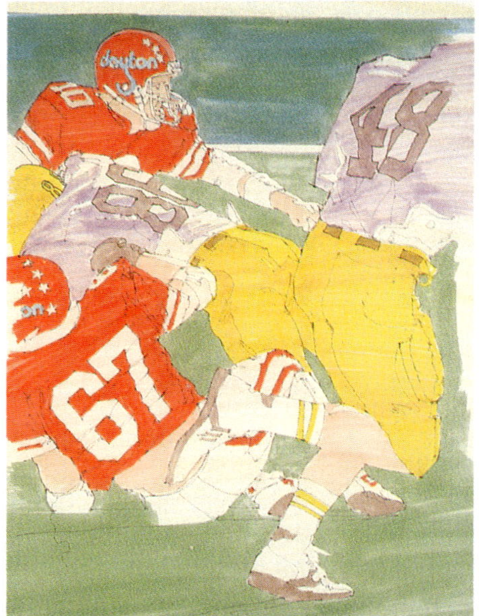

Step 1: With this project you'll capture action and motion by using your marker loosely, expressively. Before you begin pull out the full-page reproduction of this image that follows Project 3. 1) Start the rendering by applying a base tone across the page with sweeping strokes. Working wet-on-wet with broad nibs, intersperse loose horizontal strokes of brick white and cream. 2) When the base tone dries, fill in all exposed skin with a light flesh fine point. 3) Apply apple blossom to the helmets using a fine point. Keep color outside of the letters. 4) Fill in "Dayton" and part of the chin strap with a nonphoto blue fine point. Color in the white jerseys, pants, numbers, and uniform trim using warm 10% gray.

Step 2: 1) Using horizontal strokes, apply apple blossom to the Dayton players' jerseys and pant stripes using, respectively, a broad nib and a fine point. 2) With the same horizontal strokes, apply canary yellow to the opposing team's pants and helmet. In order to convey action, you *want* the strokes to show. Fill in stripes on their socks. 3) Fill in the opposing team's numbers and belts, the bottoms of all shoes, and the glove on the front Dayton player's hand with warm 40% gray. 4) Stroke nonphoto blue across the top of the page, letting some undertone show through.

Step 3: 1) Deepen the red jerseys, as well as the pant and shoe stripes, with scarlet lake. Use a fine point and allow some space between strokes. 2) Glaze in a layer of beige on all flesh and the shaded areas of the yellow pants and helmet. 3) To show shadowing on the white jerseys, streak in light violet using a fine point. 4) Fill in around the players using broad, sweeping strokes of lime green. Be sure to cover the top blue area. At this point, the illustration should begin to have an action feel from all the horizontal strokes.

PROJECT 2: *CONTINUED*

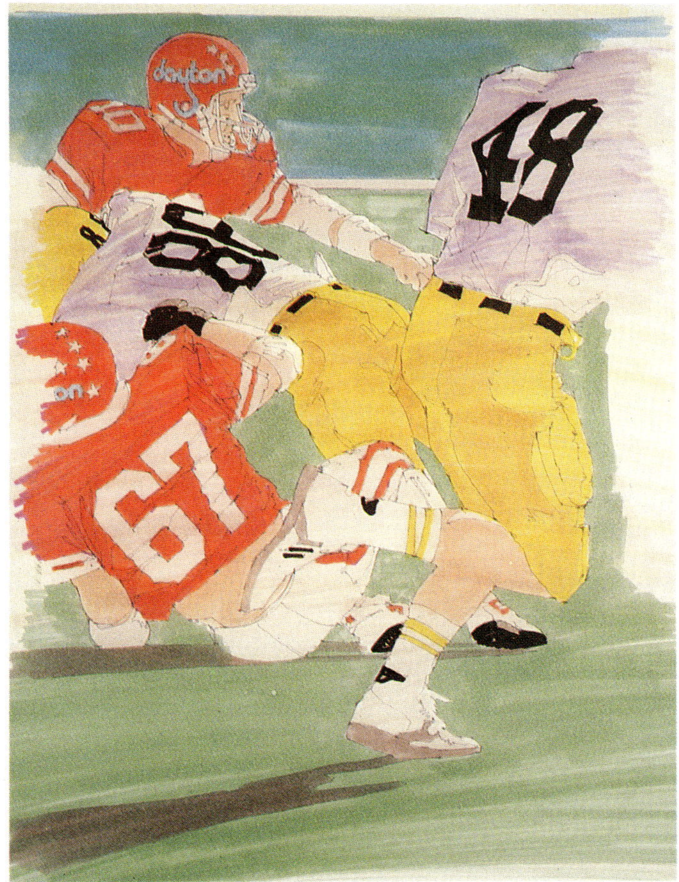

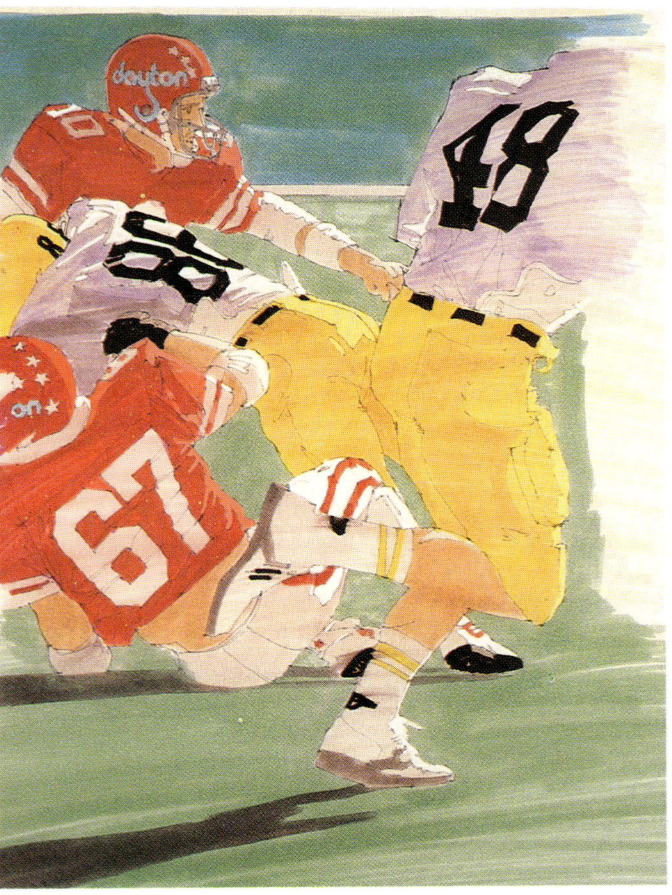

Step 4: 1) Lay cranberry in over all the red. Apply it loosely with a fine point. Again, let the horizontal strokes and some of the underneath color show. 2) Run warm 20% gray over all the figures (clothing and flesh) to neutralize color. Use a broad nib for these horizontal strokes, which will give the effect of a large shadow falling gently across the playing field. Feel free to overlap strokes, but don't try to block in a solid tone. Work loosely. 3) Fill in the cast shadows on the Astroturf with a fine-point 40% warm gray. 4) Cover all flesh tones with another layer of beige, then apply it to the shaded side of the yellow pants. 4) Use a fine-point black to fill in numbers, plus details on the shoes and their bottoms.

Step 5: 1) Stroke another horizontal layer of warm 20% gray over the players to deepen the overall shadows. 2) Fill in shadows on the turf and face mask with warm 60% gray. 3) Apply sand to all flesh to bring out the warmth. 4) Deepen shadows on the red with cranberry. These fine strokes will also intensify the color. 5) The final touches will be painted on in designer's gouache using a no. 0 brush. Mix brilliant yellow with Dr. Martin's Bleed Proof White; then, using the example as your guide, paint highlights on the yellow helmets and pants. Next, mix grenadine with the same white and apply to all red highlight areas. In both cases there should be enough contrast between the paint and the marker to show light and dark.

PROJECT 3

RENDERING A SLEEK SPORTS CAR

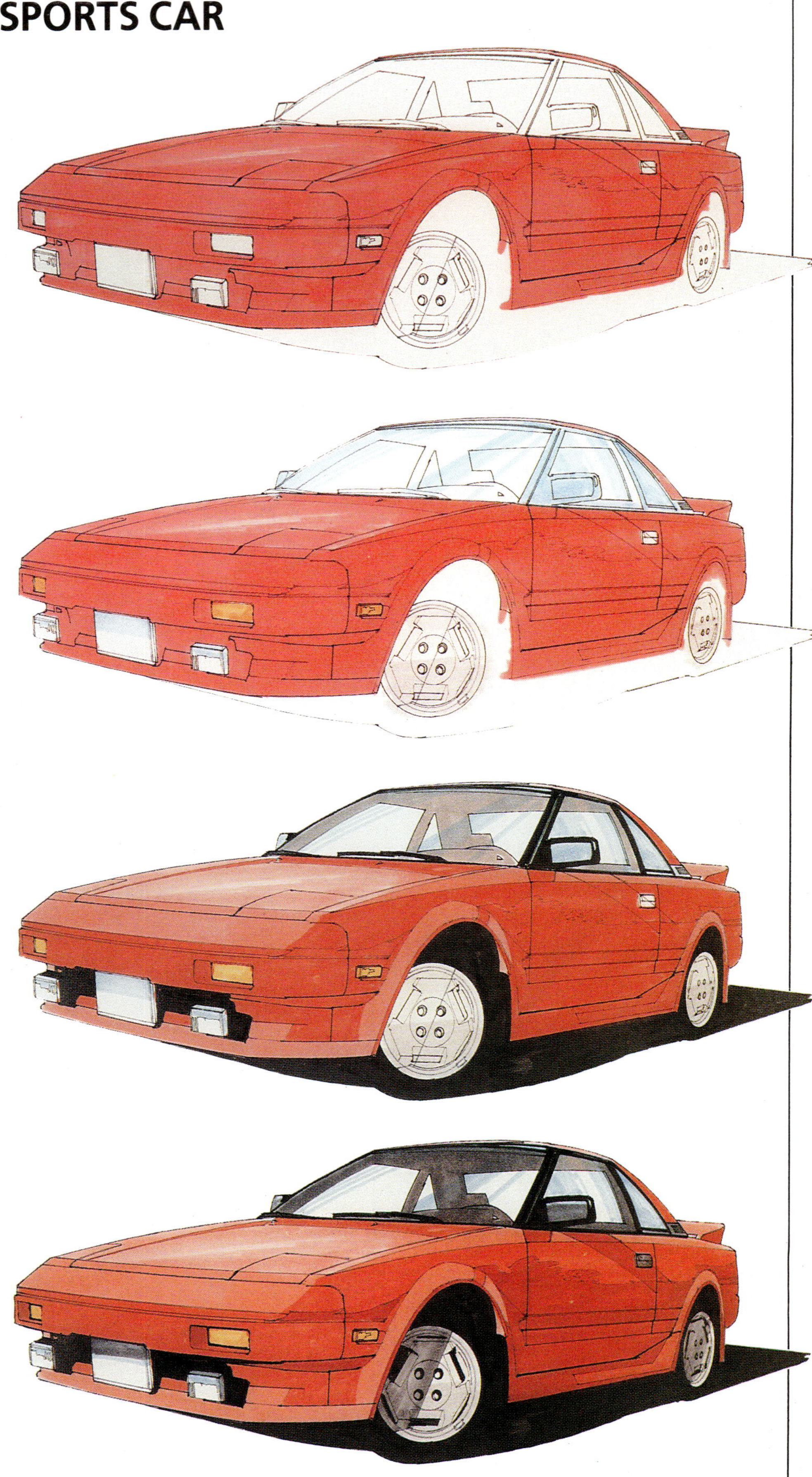

Step 1: In this final project you'll render a car's painted surfaces, glass, and matte aluminum trim. Notice that the glass is transparent in areas to show the interior. The aluminum will be clean, but not highly reflective. First make certain the full-page reproduction of this image is nearby for easy reference. Begin with the painted surface. Cover the body with apple blossom. Use a fine point for the outline and tight areas, then a broad nib for larger areas. Do not allow pigment to bleed out beyond the body or into the windshield, wheels, passenger compartment, fog lights, turn signals, or license plate.

Step 2: 1) Using a fine point, fill in the wheels with cool 10% gray. 2) Working wet-on-wet, apply cool 30% gray to the lower half of each wheel.
3) Since the sky is reflected into glass, stroke nonphoto blue onto the windshield, fog lights, and driver's window with a fine point. 4) Also apply blue to the mirrors and window molding.
5) Fill in the turn signal and parking lights using an orange fine point.
6) Apply another layer of apple blossom to the shadowed portion of the car body.

Step 3: 1) With the fine point of a cool 50% gray, fill in the trim and molding inside the passenger area. 2) Create definition on the body's shaded side with a fine-point layer of scarlet lake.
3) Take a black fine point and carefully fill in the tires, wheel wells, and shadow under the car, then the area around the fog lights, and license plate. 4) Still using the black fine point, fill in the wipers, mirrors, window trim, and molding. Use a French curve as a guide around the molding.

Step 4: 1) Using a cool 70% gray fine point, fill in the interior, window trim, door handle, mirrors (keep blue at top), plus tops of the license plate and fog lights. Next, create a shadow across the front wheel and fill in the back wheel, leaving a light area at the rear. 2) Following the horizon line reflection, stroke cranberry back along the body. Then fill in shadows under the bumper, inside the turn signals, and shooting down from the driver's mirror. 3) With a fine point, fill in black areas on the wheels and the turn signals' trim.

PROJECT 3: *CONTINUED*

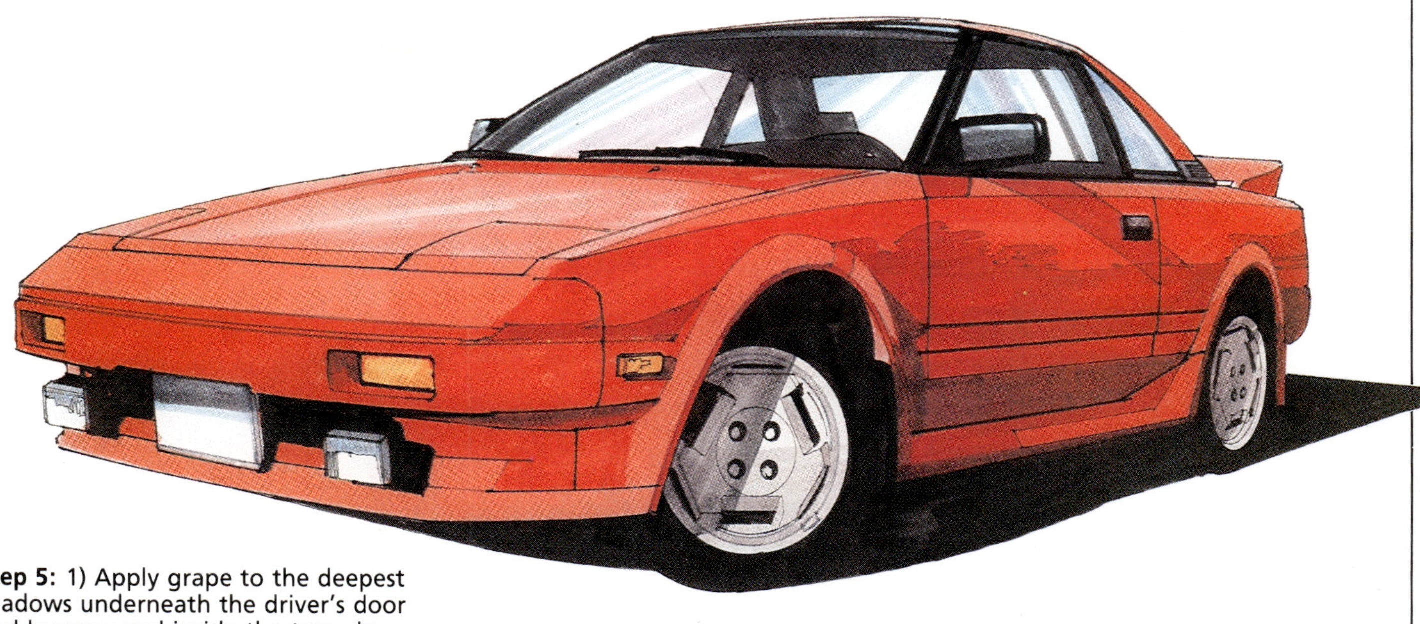

Step 5: 1) Apply grape to the deepest shadows underneath the driver's door and bumper and inside the turn signals. 2) Use a cool 70% gray fine point to carefully fill in trim, mirrors, and interior seats. 3) With cool 50% gray, add shadowing to recesses in the front wheel and turn signals, on the fog lights, and around the license plate. 4) Accent the door handle with black, and using a straightedge, rule lines on the side molding. Then fill in trim inside the car. 5) Run reflected color across the windshield and driver's window with a light violet fine point.

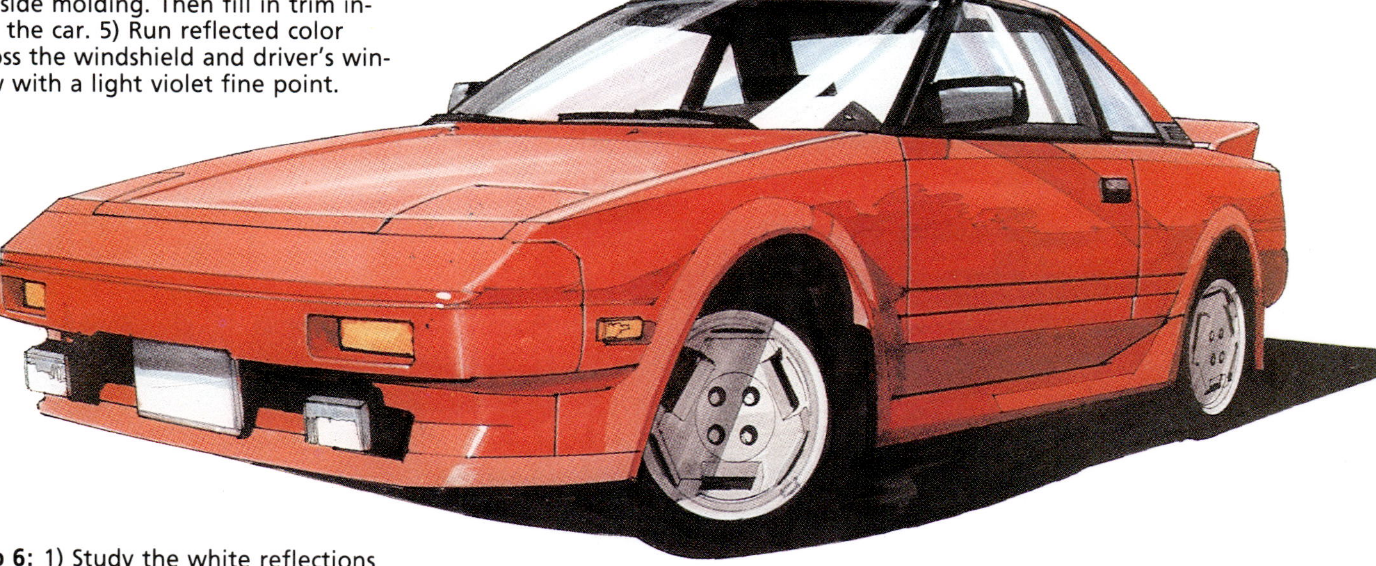

Step 6: 1) Study the white reflections on the windshield and door glass. Paint these on with Dr. Martin's Bleed Proof White and a no. 0 brush. 2) Use a sharp, white Prismacolor pencil to gently cover the black showing through the windshield's left side. Also run the pencil lightly across the top of the windshield and along the areas touching your painted highlights. 3) Complete the rendering by adding white pencil lines, struck along a French curve, around the doors, hood, signals, and headlight covers.

PROJECT 1: *FINISHED ART*

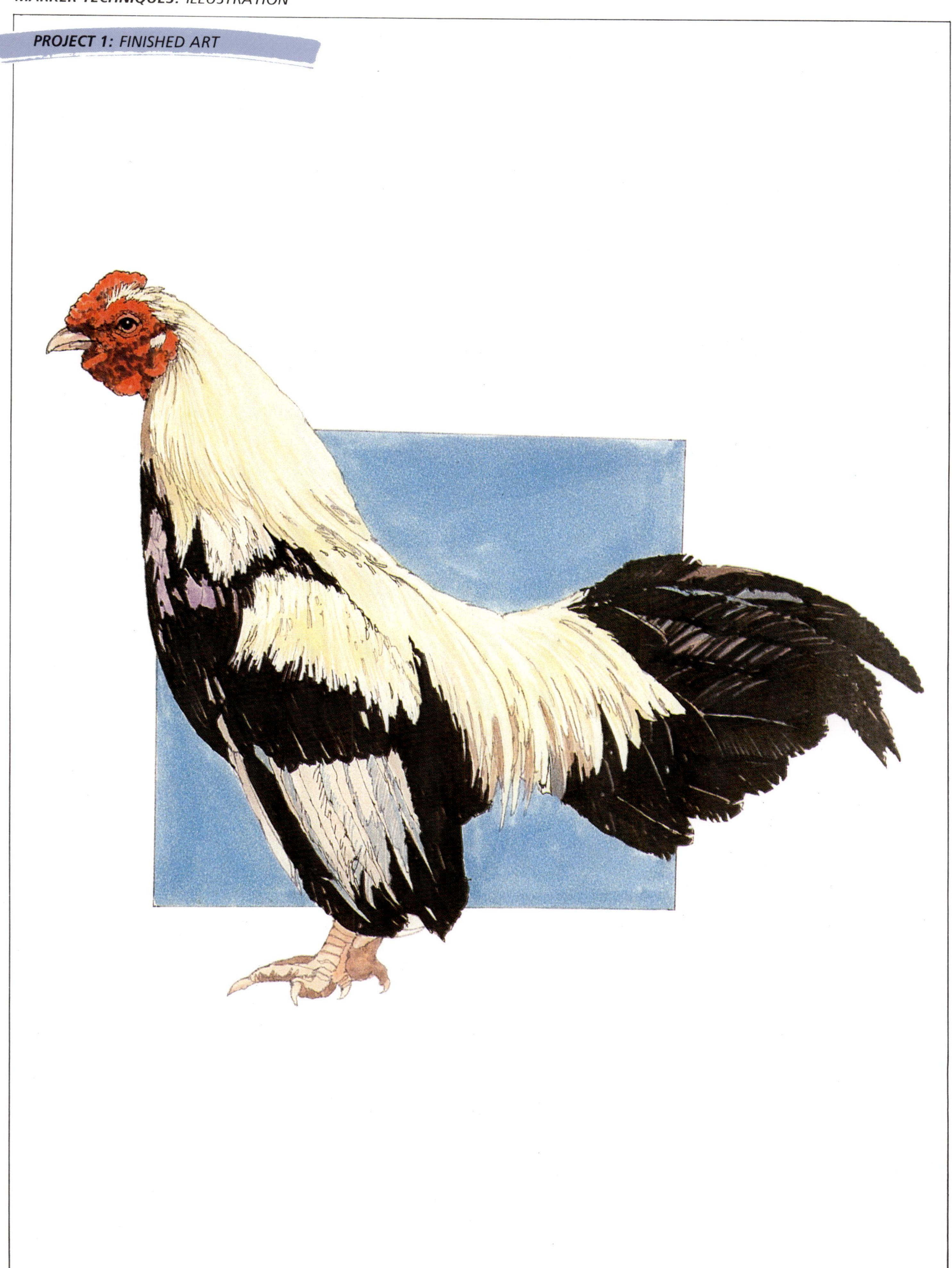

PROJECT 2: FINISHED ART

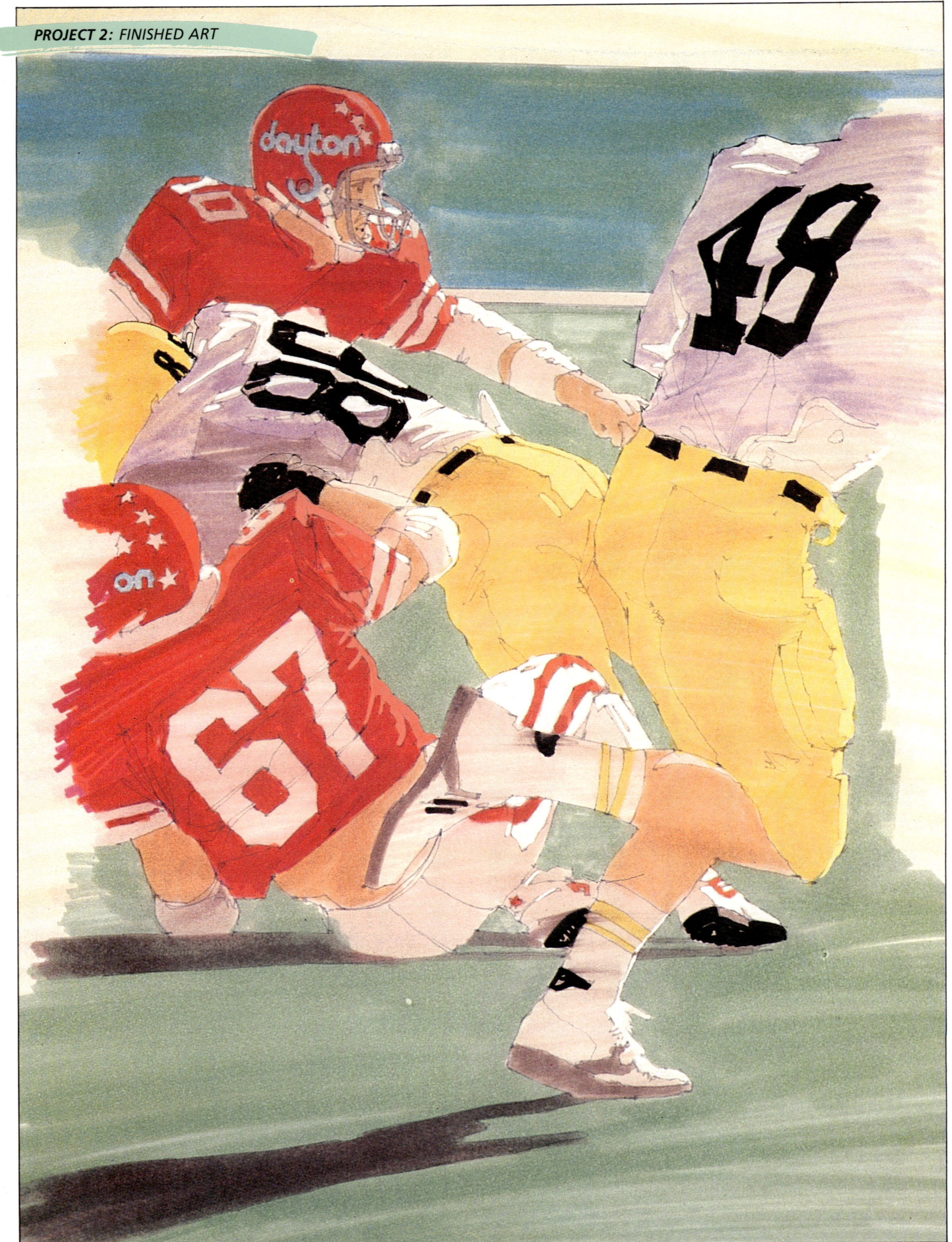

PROJECT 3: *FINISHED ART*

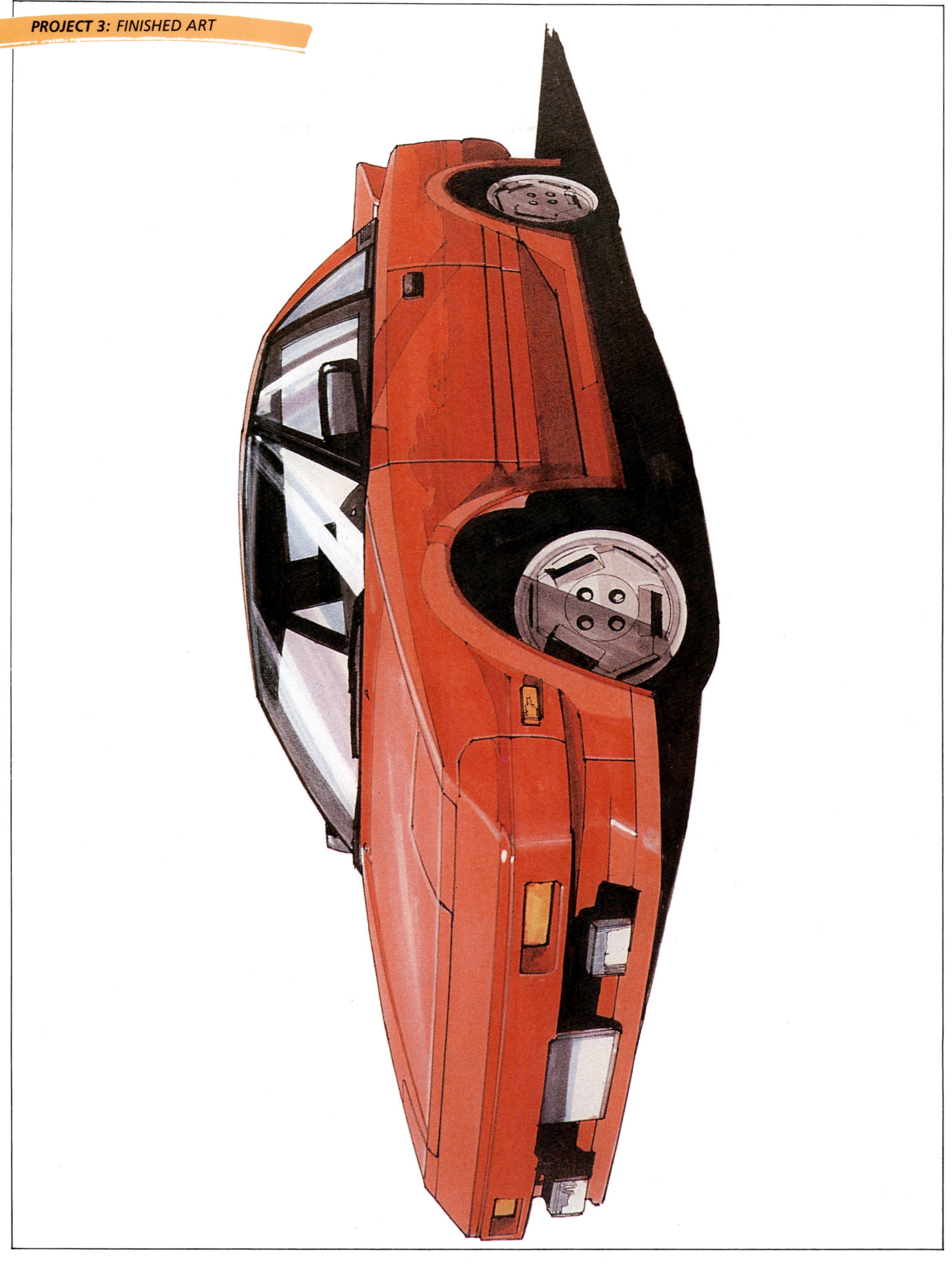

PROJECT 1: PRACTICE

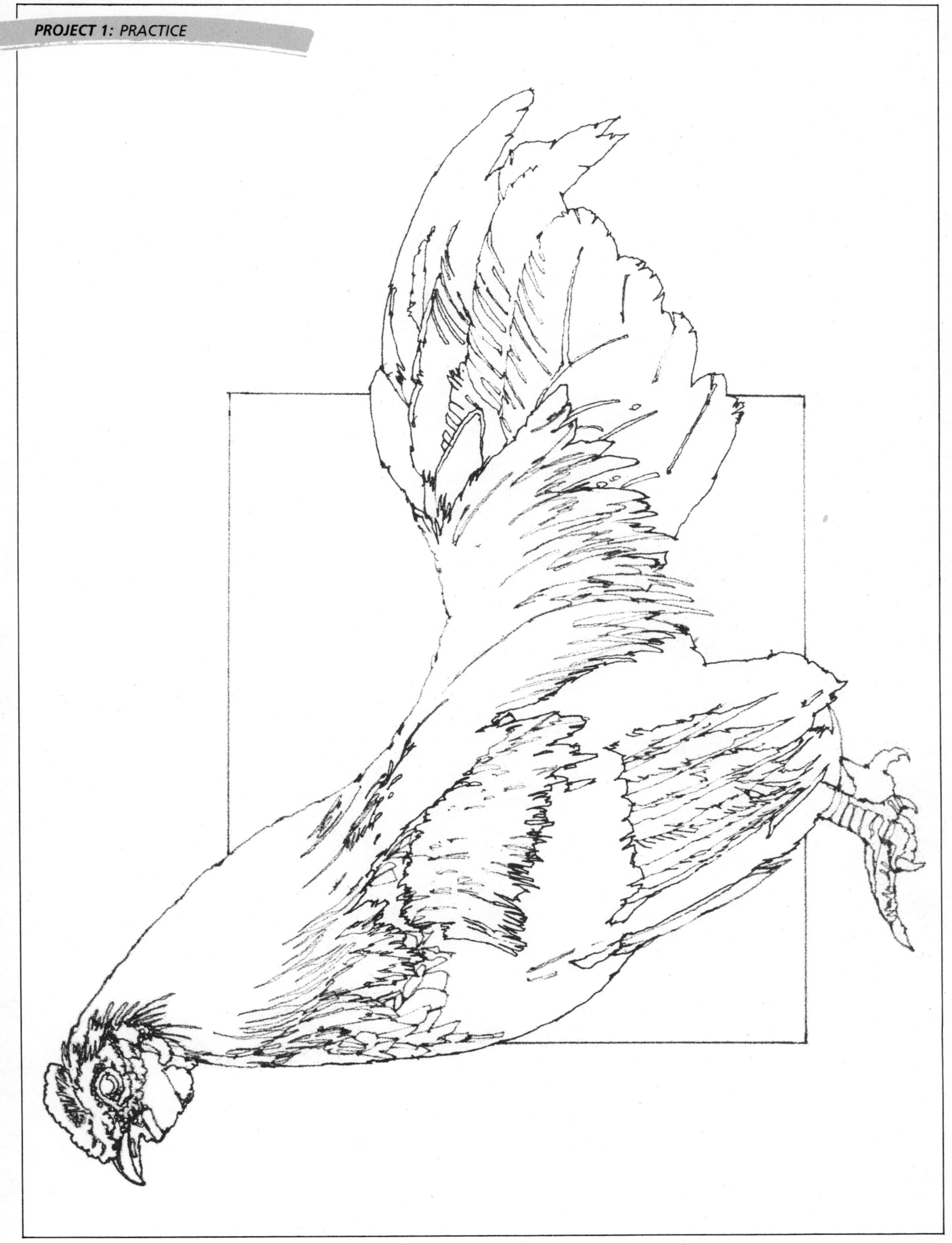

PROJECT 1: *PRACTICE*

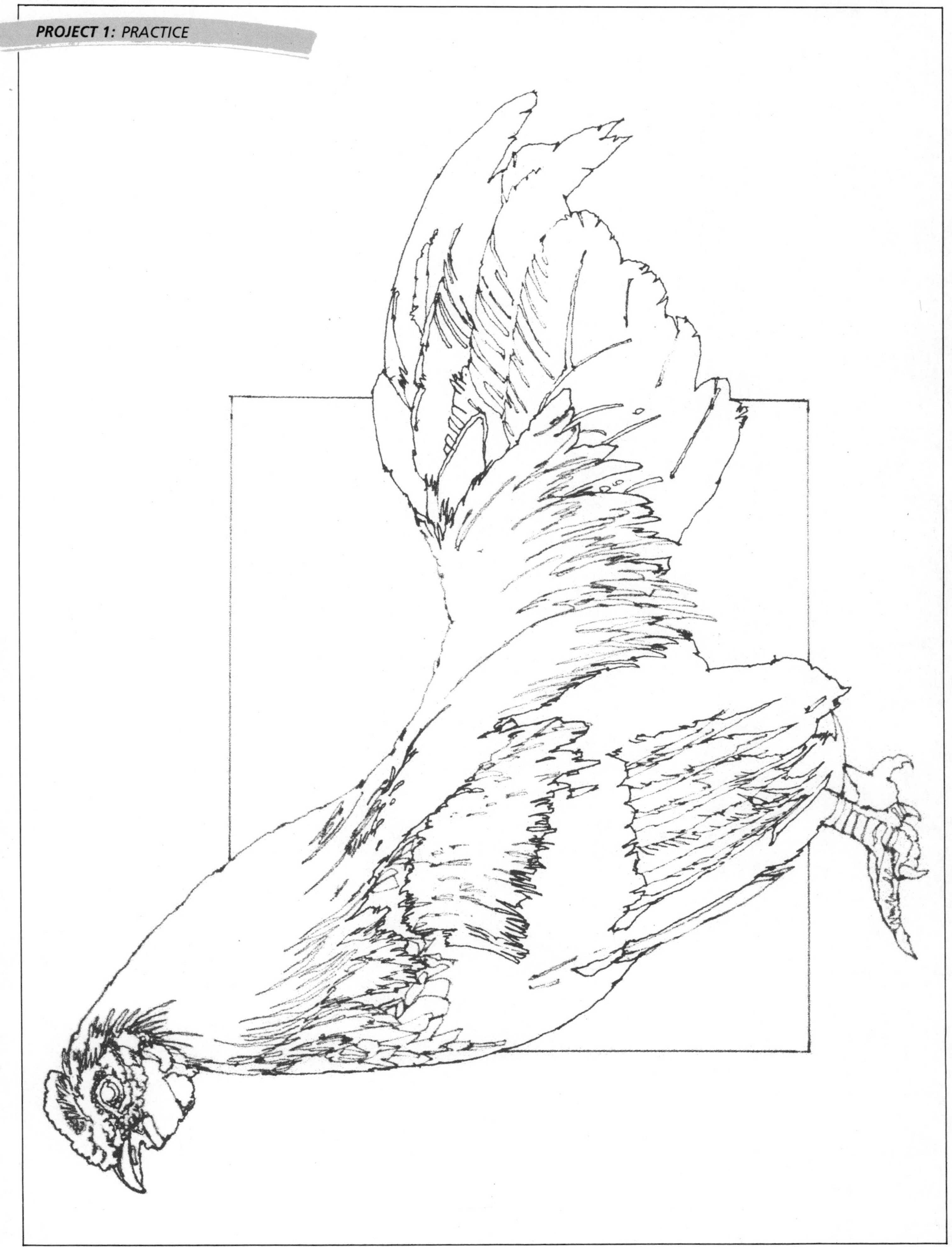

PROJECT 1: *PRACTICE*

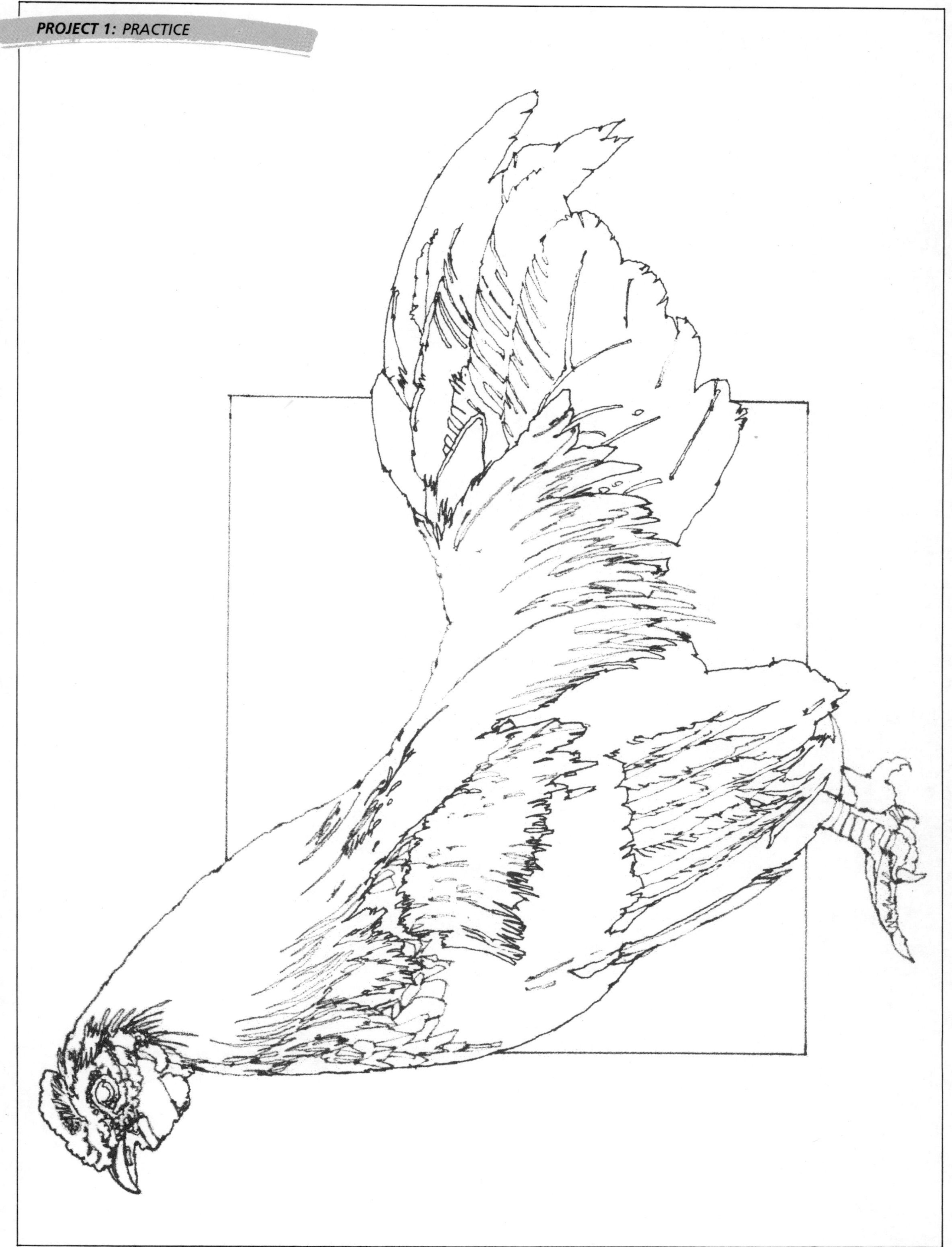

PROJECT 1: PRACTICE

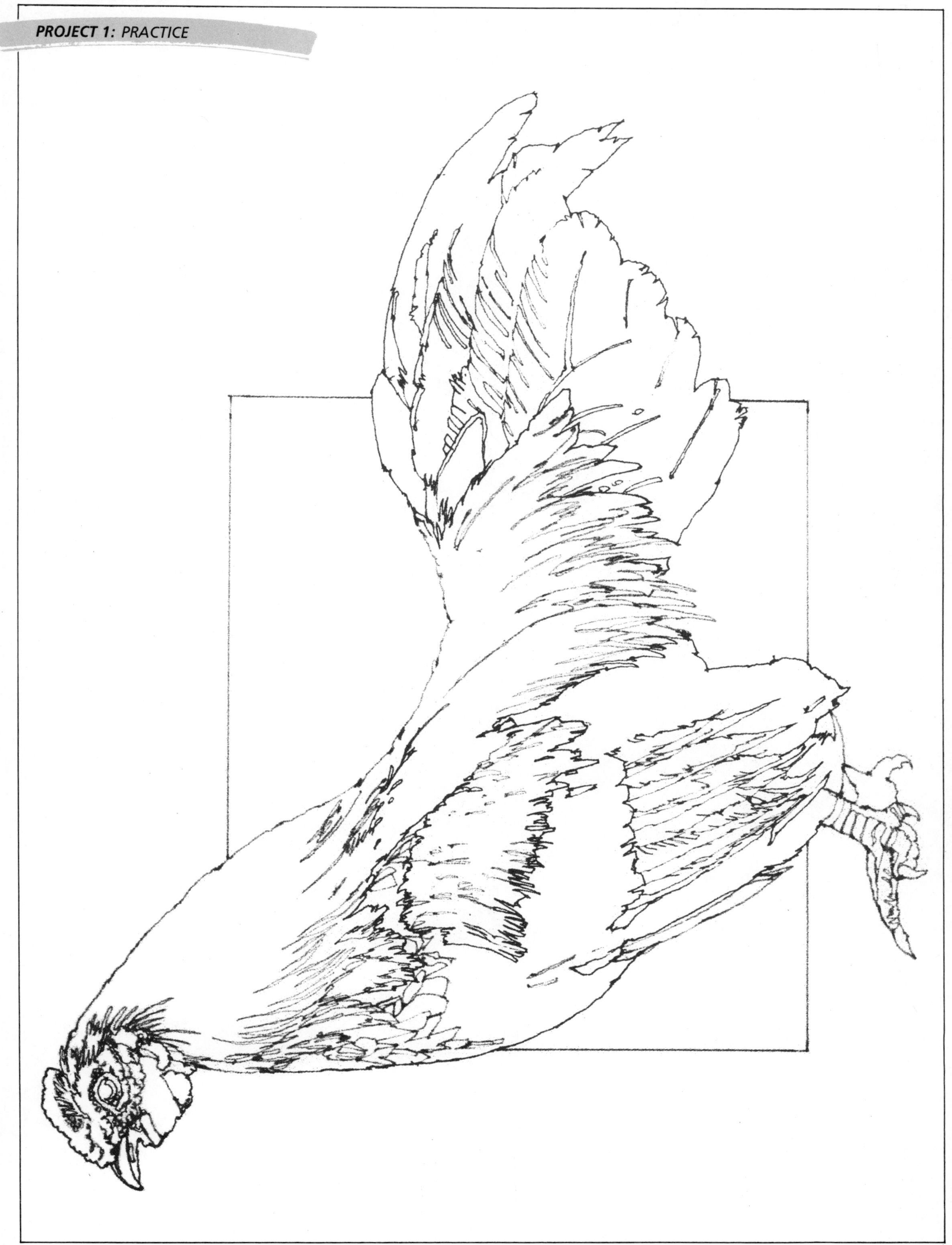

PROJECT 1: *PRACTICE*

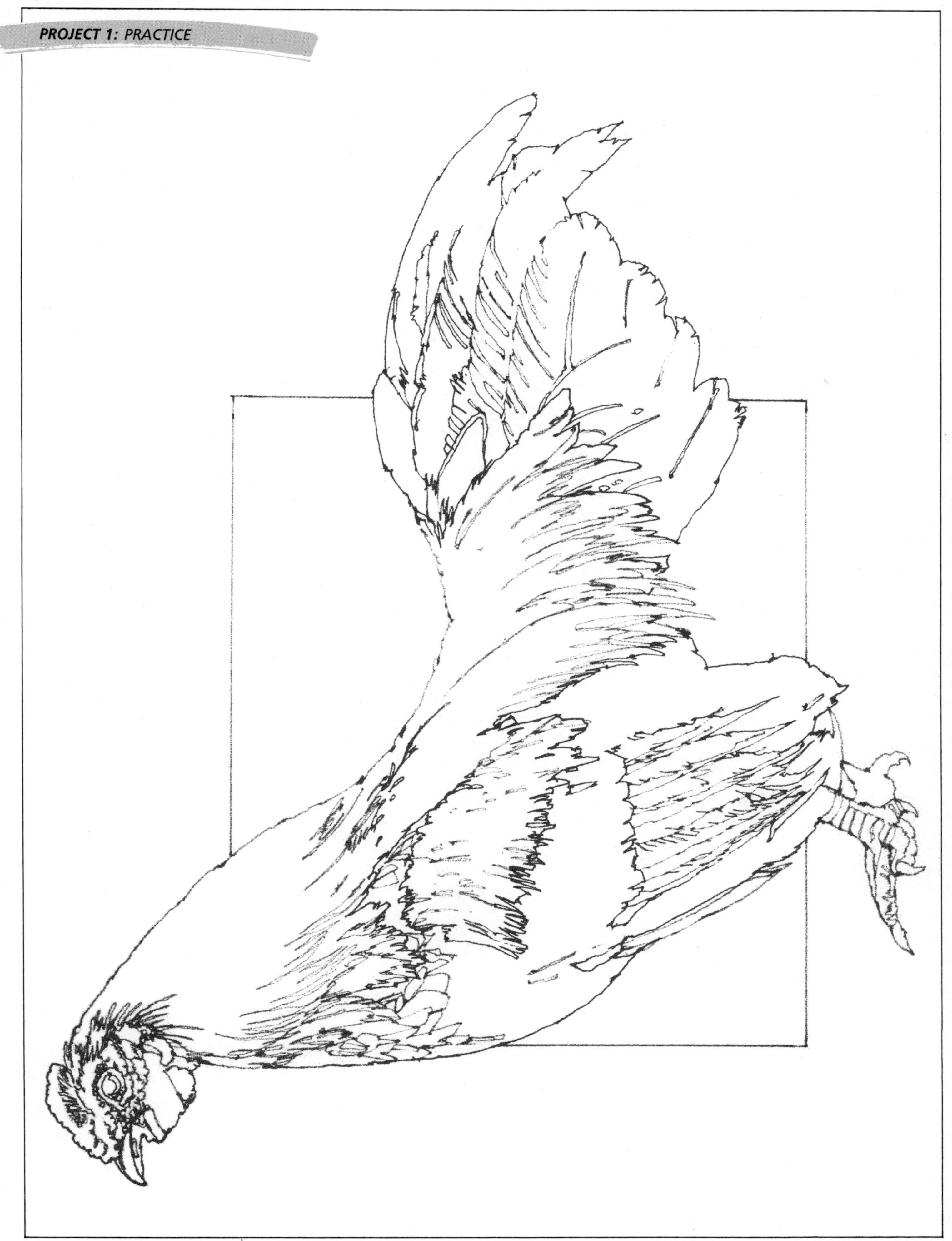

PROJECT 2: PRACTICE

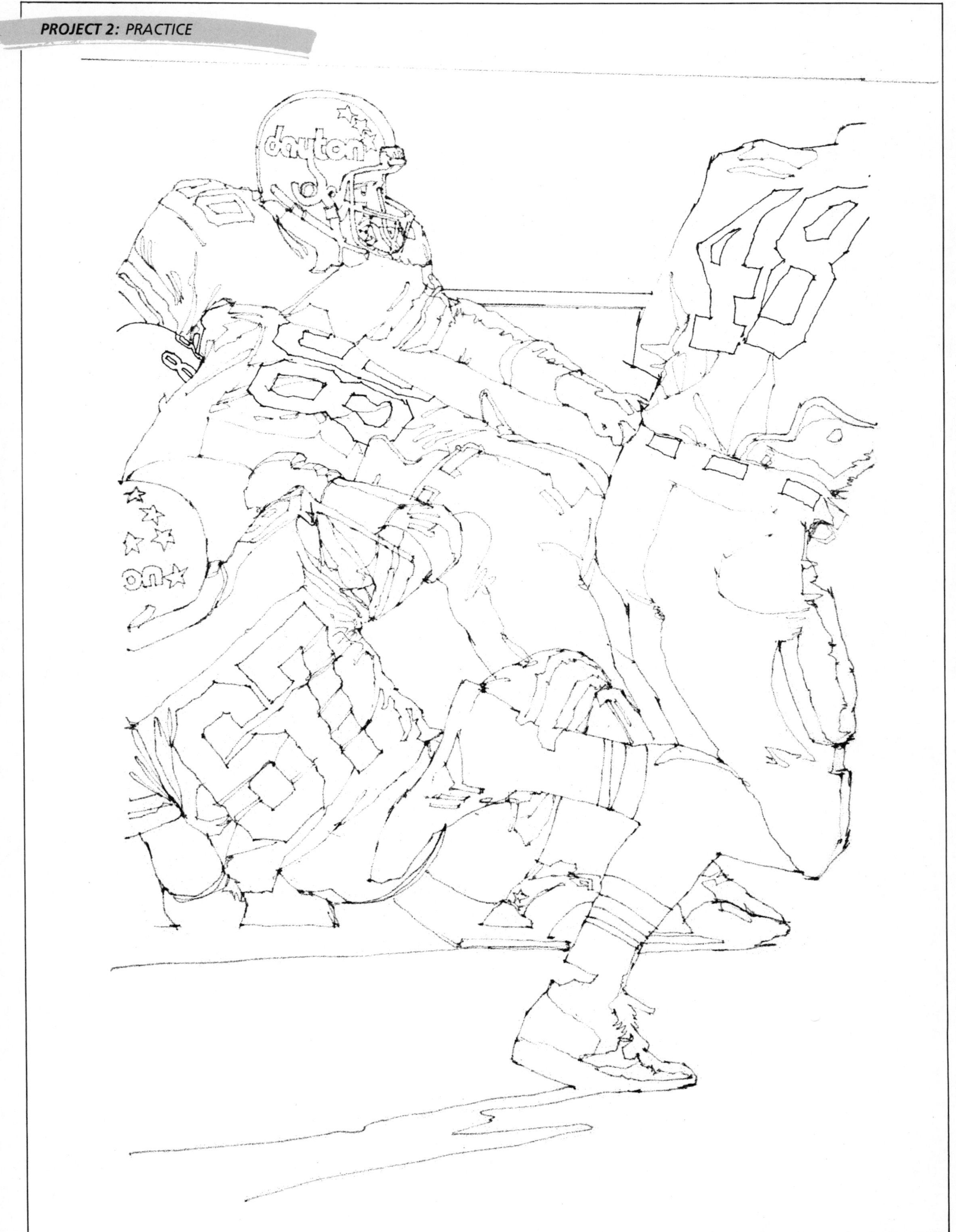

PROJECT 2: PRACTICE

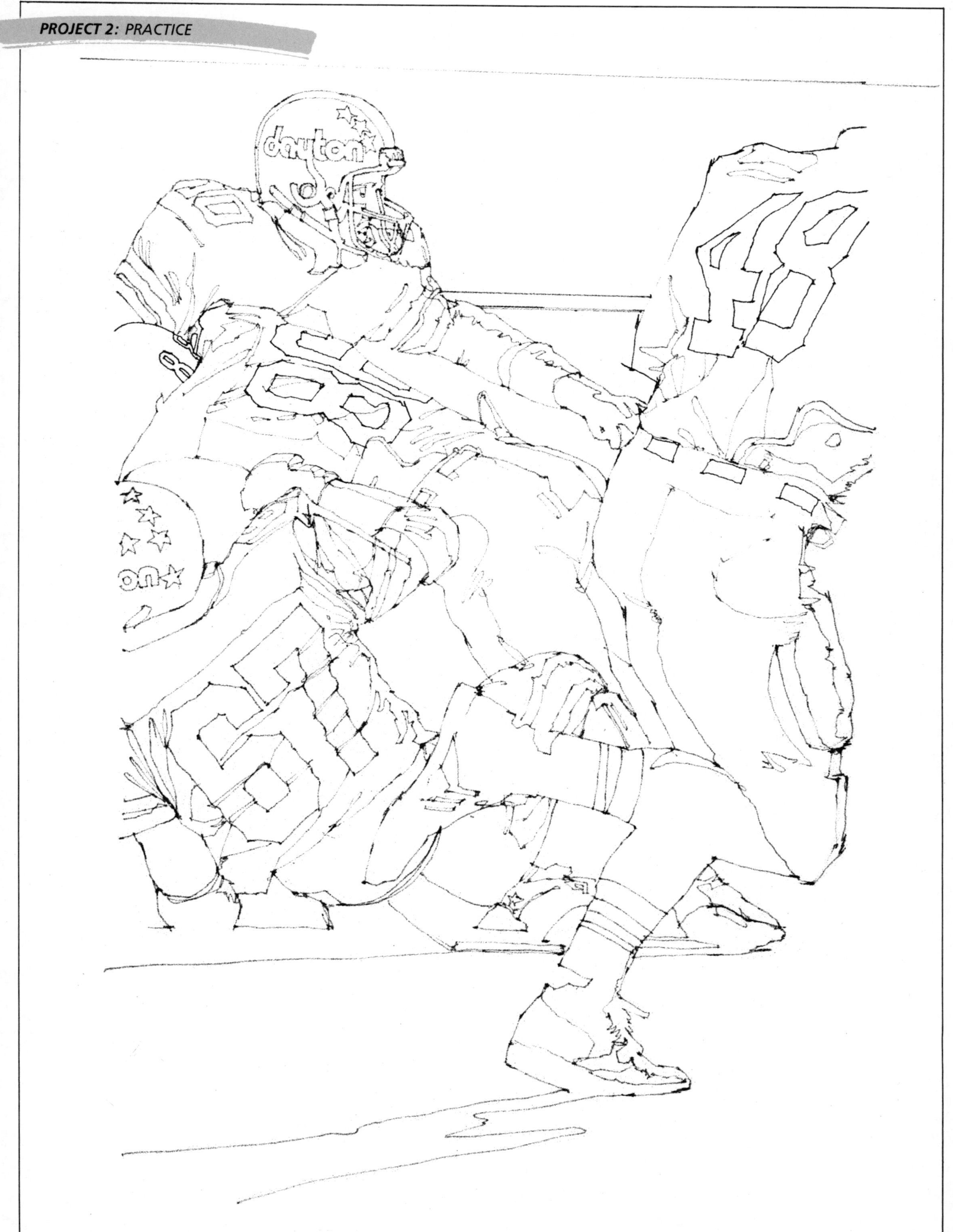

PROJECT 2: *PRACTICE*

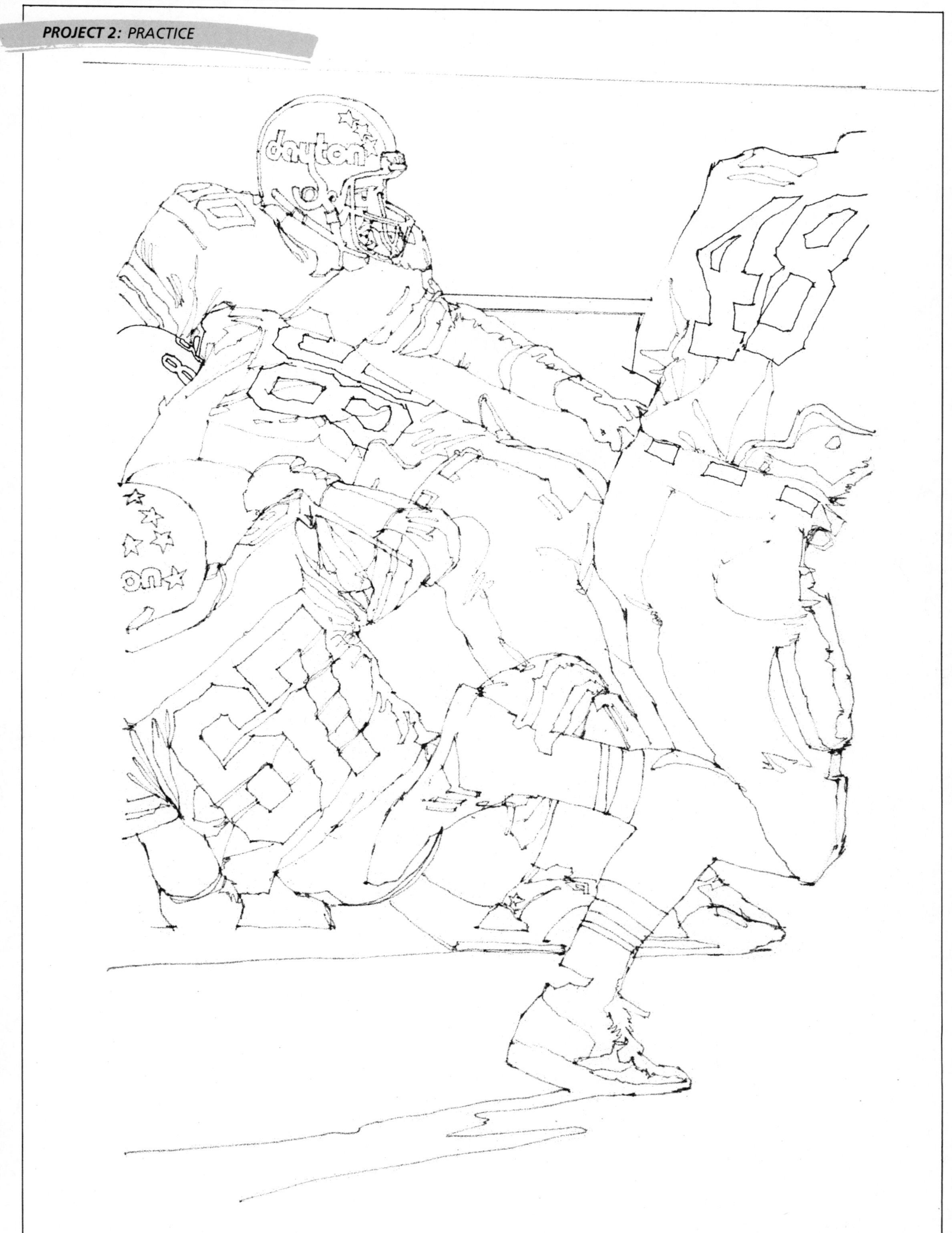

PROJECT 2: *PRACTICE*

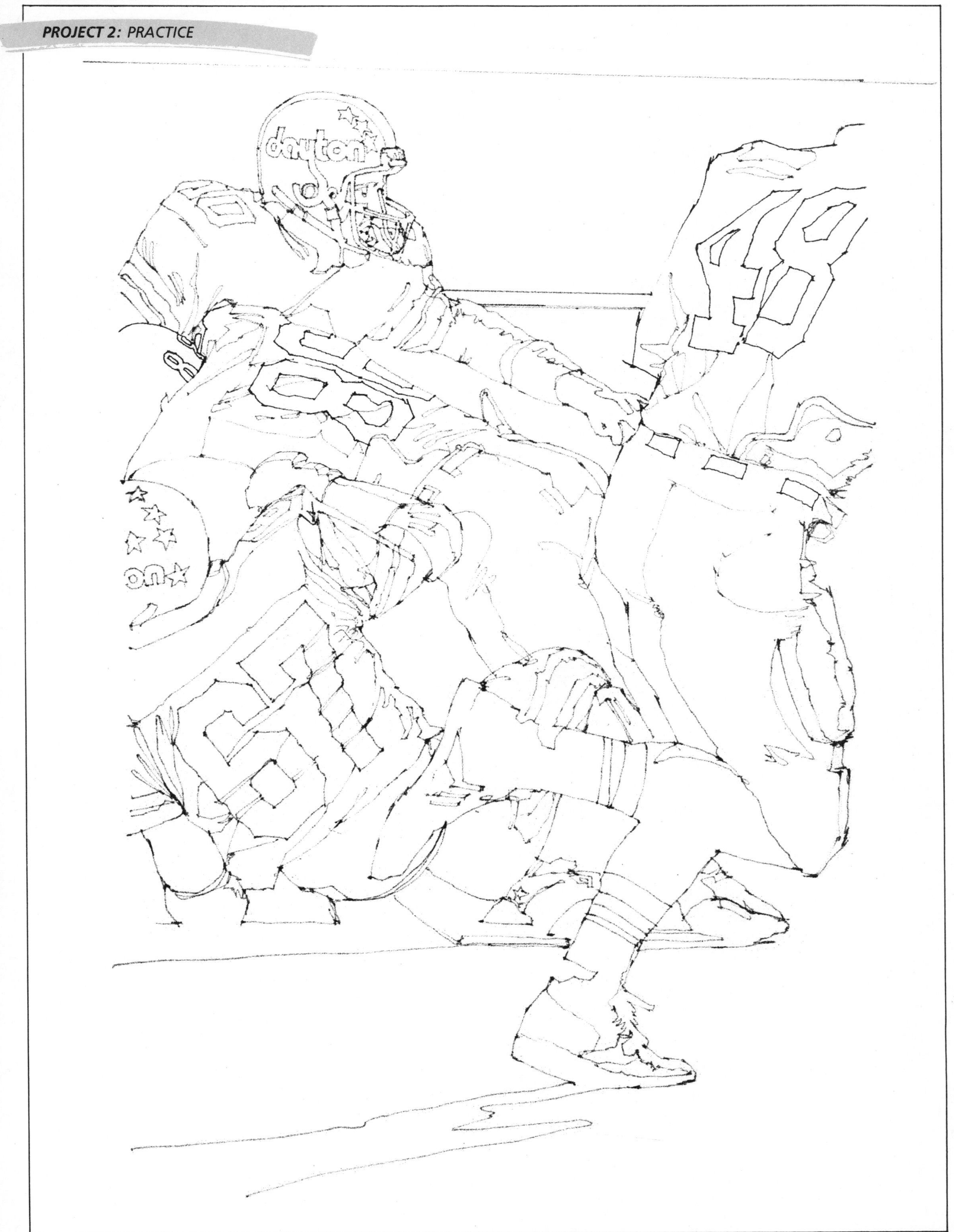

PROJECT 2: PRACTICE

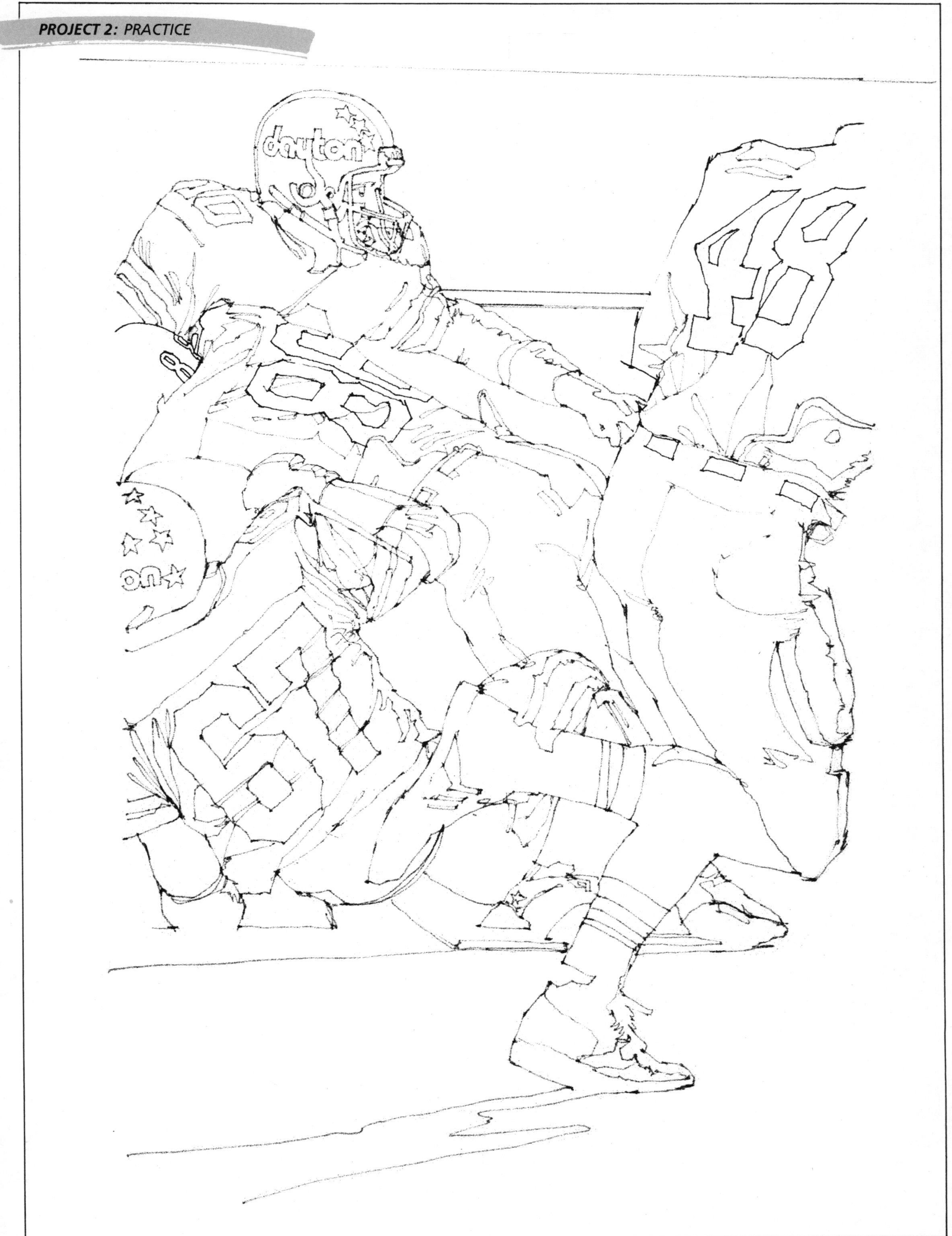

PROJECT 3: *PRACTICE*

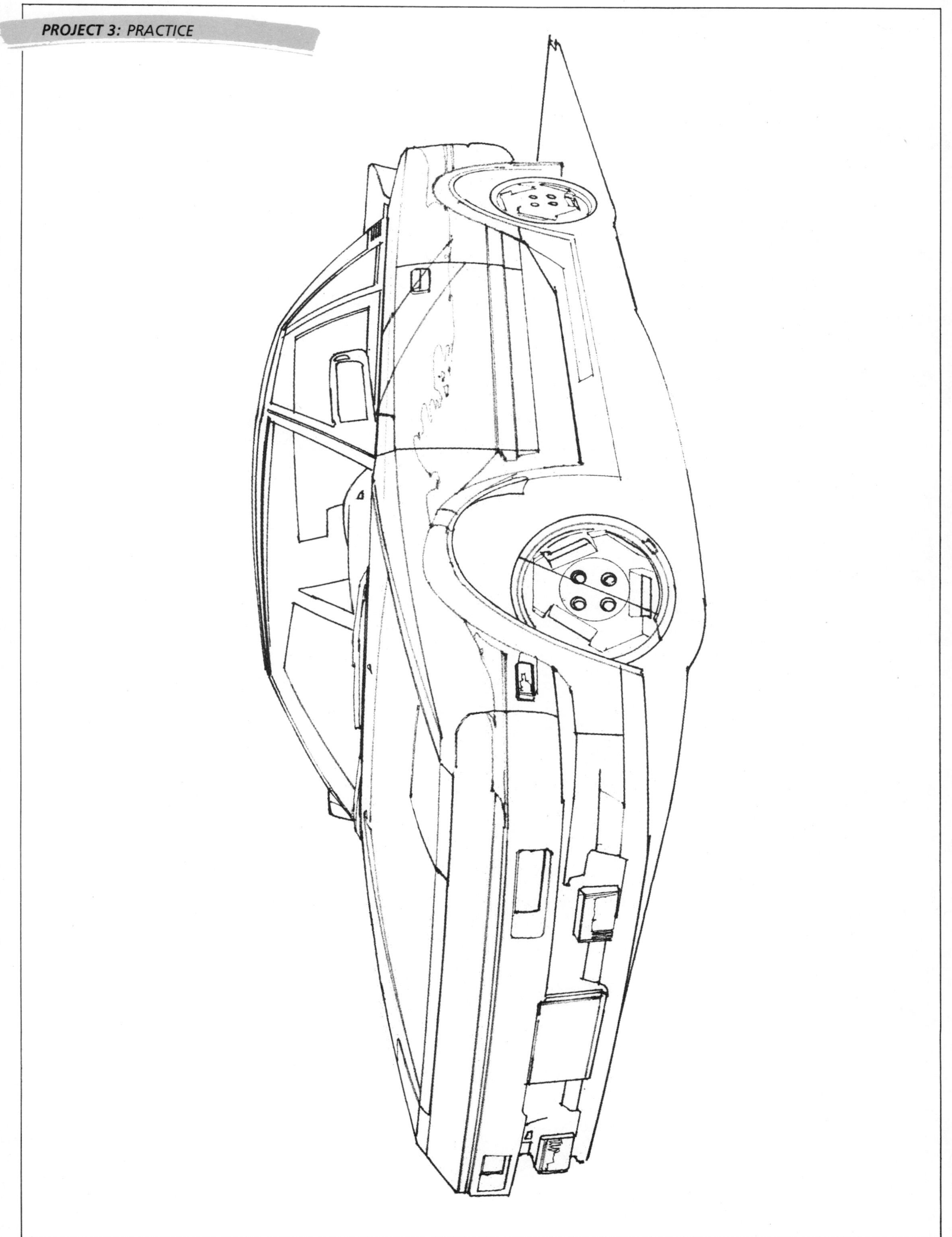

PROJECT 3: *PRACTICE*

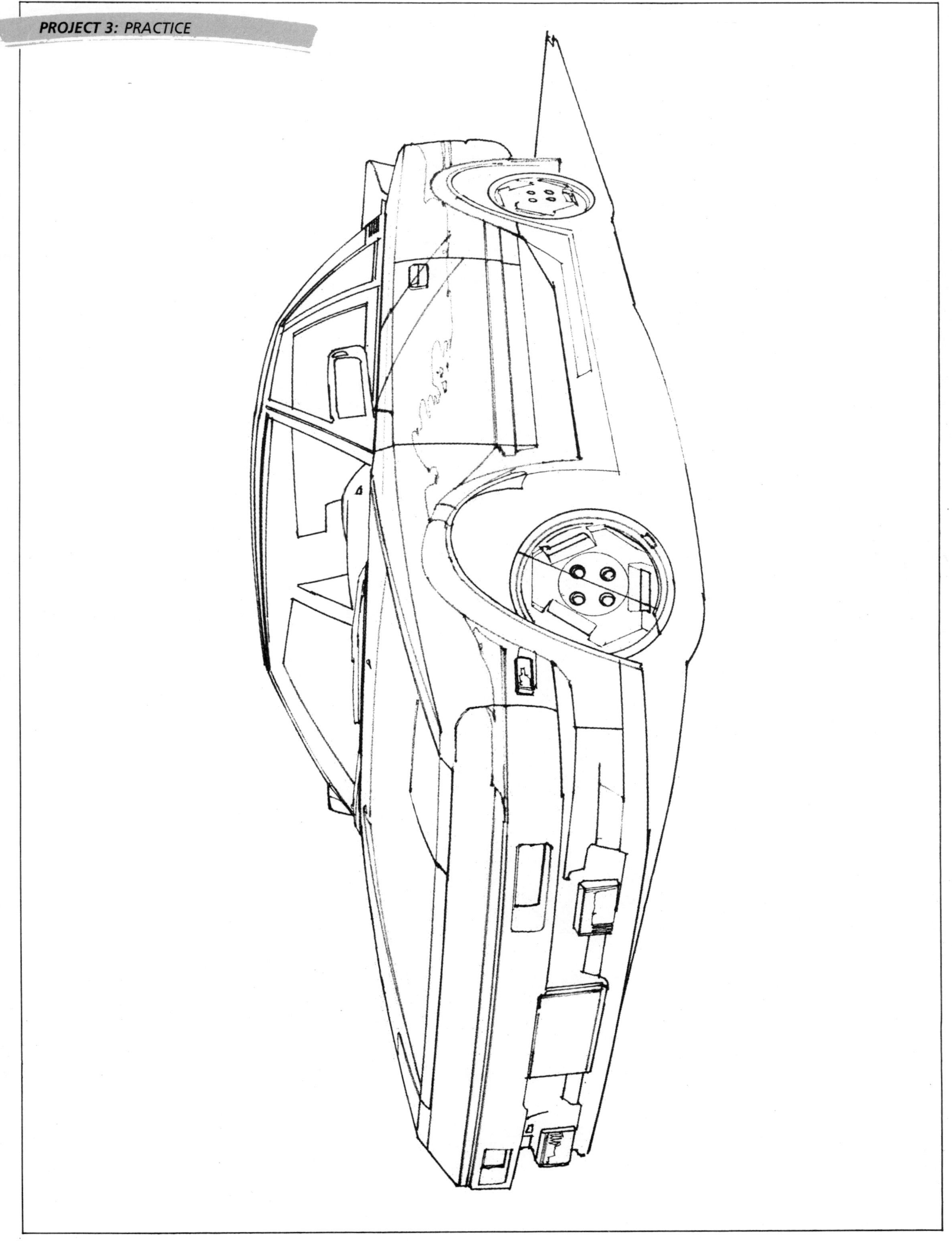

PROJECT 3: PRACTICE

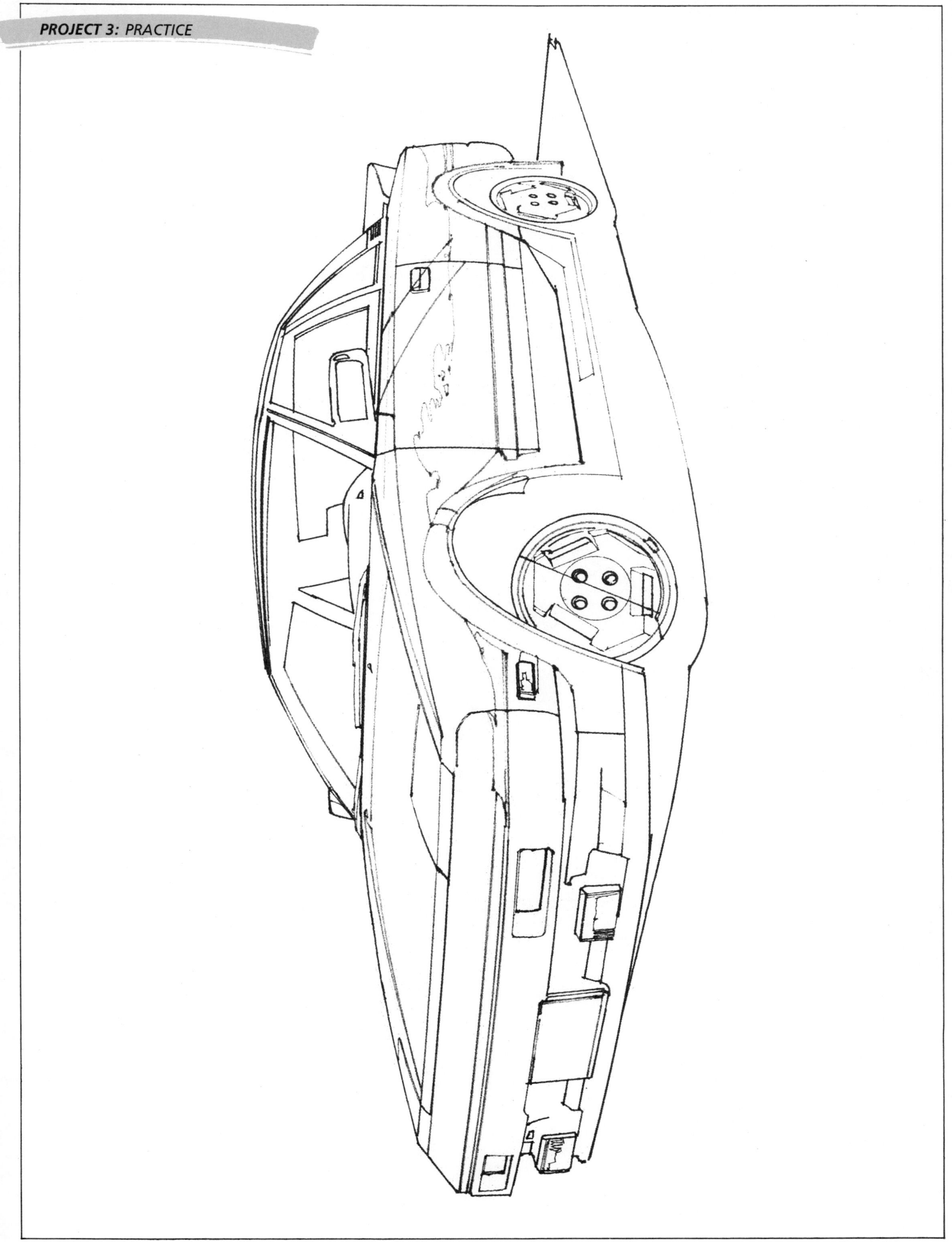

PROJECT 3: PRACTICE

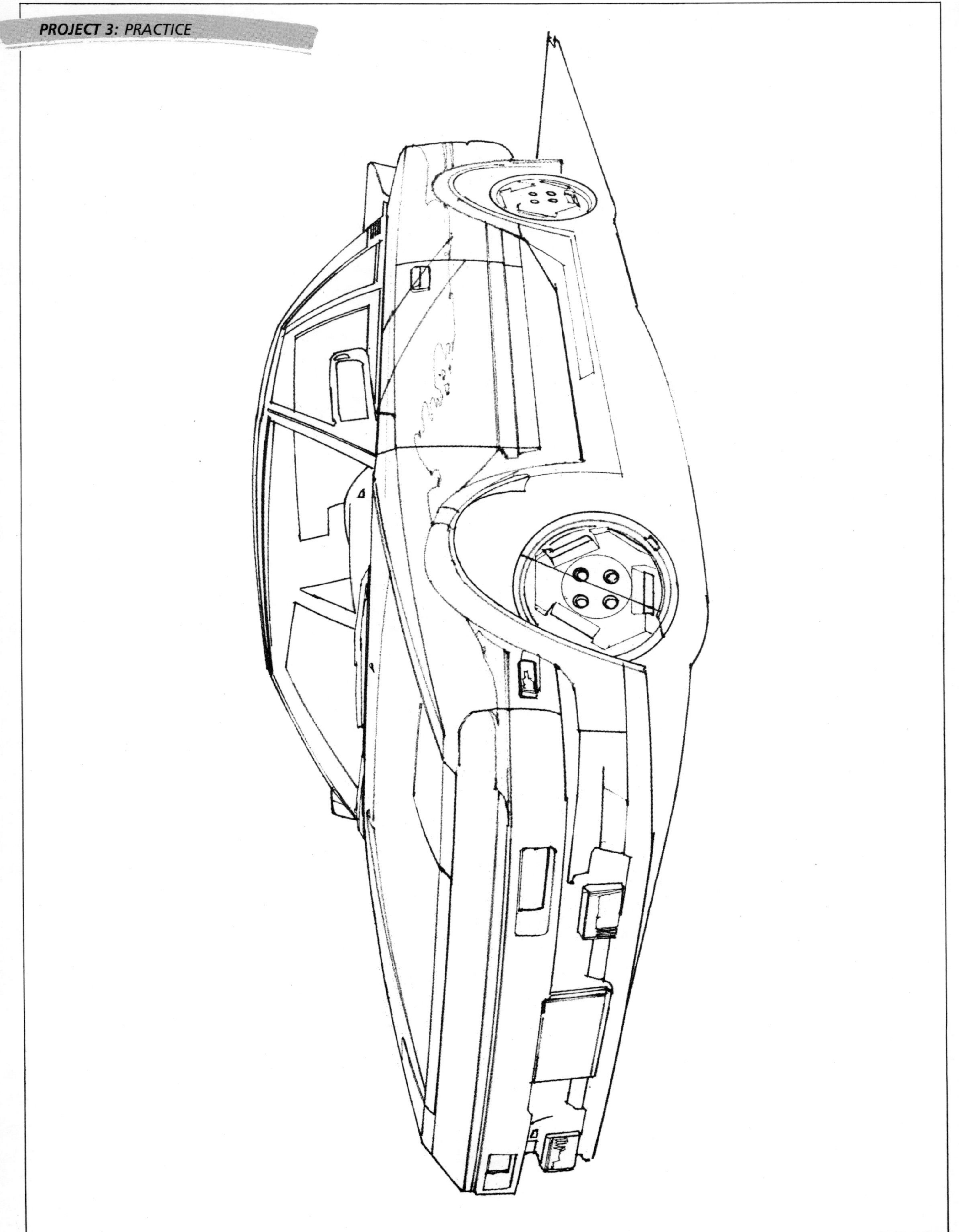

PROJECT 3: *PRACTICE*

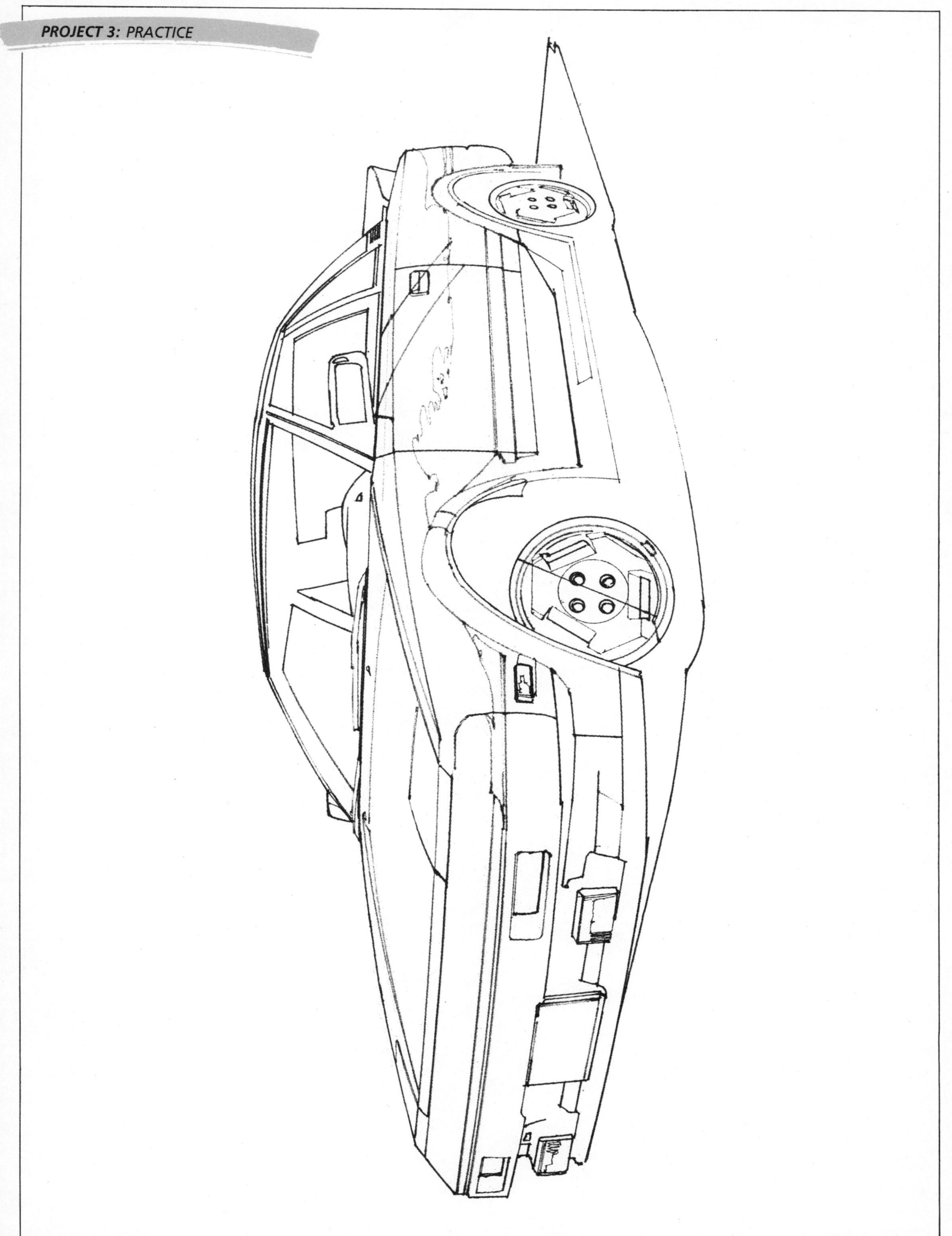

PROJECT 3: PRACTICE

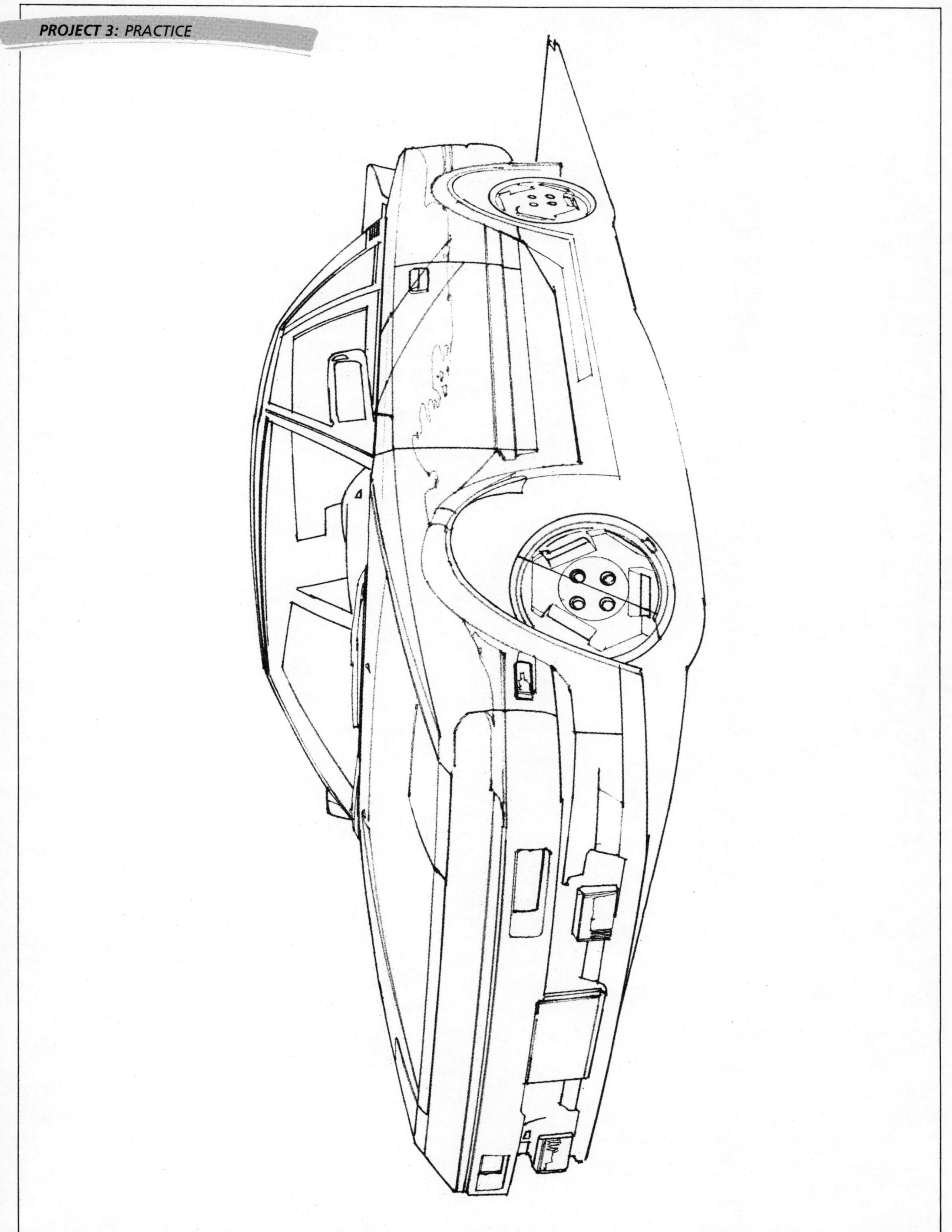